AF539479

Pakistan
In Search of Identity

Pakistan
In Search of Identity

Mubarak Ali

PAKISTAN IN SEARCH OF IDENTITY
Mubarak Ali

First Published in India 2011

ISBN 978-93-5002-099-9

Published by
AAKAR BOOKS
28 E Pocket IV, Mayur Vihar Phase I, Delhi 110 091
Phone: 011 2279 5505 Telefax : 011 2279 5641
aakarbooks@gmail.com; www.aakarbooks.com

Composed by
Limited Colors, Delhi 110 092

Printed at
Mudrak, 30 A Patparganj, Delhi 110 091

Contents

Foreword

Throughout the course of her history since independence, Pakistan has faced a persistent crisis of identity. Seldom can one find a country in the comity of nations whose intelligentsia and often the common people be seen speculating about the basis and rationale of their country. In the case of Pakistan, it is a common observation that our intelligentsia spares a major part of its time and the newspapers and periodicals spend a lot of their space on discussing the questions such as why did the country come into being? What purpose has it served? What can ensure its survival? Will it hold itself together against all divisive and centrifugal tendencies? Expressed in others words, Pakistan has for long suffered from an existential crisis.

Soon after independence, Pakistan had to opt for one of the two paths for its future identity. One was to realise that though the Two Nation theory was useful and conducive for the realisation of a Muslim state in the subcontinent (thereby negating the Congress's assertion of a united Indian nationalism), the theory came to outlive itself once that country came into being. A continued assertion at the Two Nation theory would have implied that in future, a minority within Pakistan could have made a similar claim of separate nationhood as did the Muslims in India. Moreover, the continued assertion of the Two Nation theory would have anchored Pakistan in the pre-partition situation preventing it from dissociating itself from a communal past and building itself on original and future-oriented foundations.

The other choice was to continue to assert the permanence of the Two Nation theory in which case Pakistan was likely to permanently need India as an essential reference for its nationhood, and a *raison d'etre* for its existence. Moreover, the Two Nation theory would have created cleavages in Pakistan's politics and would have cut its society to the core.

Certainly, the wiser ones among the Pakistani leadership, particularly, Muhammad Ali Jinnah, the founder of Pakistan, opted for the former. In his famous 11 August 1947 speech, he proclaimed his vision of Pakistan and presented the noble idea that by shunning the differences of caste, creed, language and ethnicity, we could build a truly Pakistani nation. He also highlighted the importance of the neutrality of the state with reference to the citizens suggesting that it was only after the ending of the angularities of the majority community and the minority community that a true concept of nationhood could be evolved. Unfortunately, overlooking the forthright and enlightened perception of nationhood as articulated by the founder of the country, his successors adopted the latter course preventing a positive and constructive view of nationhood. As a result, Pakistan did not succeed in evolving a true national identity free from the pre-independence hangover of communal antagonism.

Pakistan's malaise did not end here; unfortunately, the ruling elite of the country failed to evolve a consensus among them over the crucial political issues, and in the absence of this consensus, they decided to use religion to court the support of the people and provinces who were seeking their rights and their rightful place in the country. Islam was thus designated as the basis of Pakistan's identity. Once Islam was demoted from the status of a religion to that of an ideology, the pertinent question could be raised as to what kind of a state with Islam as its ideology would take shape and who would determine whether or not the state had become truly Islamic. This gave a pre-eminence to the class of clergy who in the context of the traditional religious society of the country asserted its decisive role in statecraft. It was, therefore, suggested that the *ulema* alone could determine the validity of an Islamic law. The *ulema* also claimed that it was they who could properly interperet the teachings of Islam. The successive governments legitimised their rule through the use of Islamic slogans while the values of justice, compassion and brotherhood as professed by Islam were never translated into the state policies. It is quite understandable why this ideological engineering did not pay dividends and compelled the country to grope towards an ambiguous destination.

The author of this book, Dr. Mubarak Ali, has taken pains to investigate the multifarious ideological crises of Pakistan. Without subscribing to any preconceived notion, he analyses the issues of ideology and identity purely from historical and political points of view. His approach is objective and rational and he studies the issues of state formation in Pakistan and Pakistan's quest for nationhood in a scientific manner underlining the socio-economic causes operating behind the political events. He begins with the examination of the emergence of the Muslim consciousness about their identity in the socio-cultural environment of pre-partition India. He then moves on to examine how the issue of identity resurfaced in Pakistan after its independence. He examines the various trends, both secular and religious, which continued for years to combat each other. The policies of the state, its efforts in securing legitimacy through employing religious propaganda, the construction of an official religious ideology and the implications of all these moves also come under critical scrutiny. The author endeavors to analyse the integrating as well as separating aspects of the co-relation between religion and politics. He sheds light on the political economy of Islamisation and explains how in a growing environment of commercialisation, the politicisation of religious affiliations impacts the society in a negative way.

The views expressed in the chapters of this book would certainly invite debate and would encourage others to build up on what has been concluded here or, while contesting this, come up with better arguments and better explanations of the issues addressed here.

The author of this book deserves our thanks for addressing the above issues in a bold and rational manner. Dr. Mubarak Ali is a prolific writer who has created for himself a prominent niche among the historians of our country. In the last three decades, he has written with great persistence and courage on matters which have been rendered sensitive by the uncritical thinking prevailing in our society. Dr. Mubarak Ali has to his credit quite a few contributions which may not be overlooked by a judicious mind. First, he had the courage to take the discipline of history out of the strict confines of our so-called professional historians, most of whom have chosen to isolate their work from a wider and vibrant society. Dr. Mubarak Ali has brought history to the common people by not only shifting the focus of history from the coteries and courts to the common people but also by producing his narratives in lucid language. No wonder his writings are so popular among students, political workers and general readers. Secondly, the fact that he has indicated through his writings that a clearer historical picture may not undermine the wider and multifarious aspects of society at a given period of time has given to his historical writings an edge over those who have approached the past through the limited scope of political history. Dr. Ali's writings on culture, arts, beliefs, attitudes, behaviour, etc., together with the study of politics, gives a comprehensive and more trustworthy picture of the past. Thirdly, Dr. Mubarak Ali has off and on produced a very strong critique of official historiography and has shown its inconsistencies and tendentiousness. He is quite convincing when he suggests that once confined in an ideological straitjacket of a state, history loses its rationale and creativity; it freezes the mindset of the people rather than liberates them. Finally, Dr. Mubarak Ali has taken to history writing —or, to be more precise, his way of history writing—as a mission. He writes not only books but also produces a well received journal, titled *Tareekh,* and has been able to build a team of young historians who may not appear very influential at the moment but, given time, would certainly make themselves noticeable on the academic and intellectual landscape of the country. For years, we have lamented the absence of critical historical inquiry in our intellectual discourses but it seems that the same would not remain our fate. We see a ray of hope at the end of the tunnel, and one does not hesitate to suggest that among those who would, at the end of the day, be commended for clearing up the foggy horizon for the truthful portrayal of our history, Dr. Mubarak Ali would certainly have a prominent place.

In the production of this book, the young research staff of Pakistan Study Centre has made a useful contribution for which I remain grateful. I am particularly thankful to my young colleague Yasir Hanif for preparing the index of the book.

Dr. Syed Jaffar Ahmed
Pakistan Study Centre,
University of Karachi, Karachi

1
Consciousness of Muslim Identity in South Asia Before 1947

The question of Muslim identity in the Indian subcontinent may be analysed on the basis of social, religious, and political consciousness. Socially, the Muslim communities of India have never been united as a single cohesive entity. Their religious identity was transformed from a passive state to an active one according to the changing priorities of the ruling classes. They invoked religious sentiments when they fought against Hindu rulers and suppressed them when the *shariah* hindered their absolute rule. The concept of a Muslim political identity was a product of British rule when the electoral process, the so-called democratic institutions and traditions were introduced. British rule that created a minority complex amongst Indian Muslims and thereby a consciousness of Muslim political identity. After passing through a series of upheavals, the Muslim community shed its minority complex and declared itself a nation, asserting its separateness.

Northern India remained the centre of Muslim power, historically. The class of leading Muslim elites played an active role in determining and affirming Muslim identity according to their economic and political interests. Muslims of the other parts of India followed in their footsteps and perceived issues and problems from the point of view of northern Indian Muslims. We shall look at the changing concepts of Muslim identity in the Indian subcontinent before 1947.

Three elements were amalgamated in the making of Muslim communities in India, namely conquerors who came from the north-west, immigrants, and local converts. The conquerors and their entourage had a sense of higher rank and superiority as it was they who wielded political power. Arab, Persian, Turkish, Central Asian, and Pathan immigrants, who came to India to make careers for themselves, were treated as if they shared a common ethnic background, and were integrated with the conqueror class as the ruling elite. Local converts, on the other hand, were treated as being lower down the social ladder and never accorded an equal place in the ethnically divided Muslim society. Thus, ethnic identity was more powerful in dividing Muslim society than the religious factor was in unifying it.

We can find an example of this in *Chachnama,* which is a basic source of the history of Sindh. Muslim conquerors of Sindh are referred to in the *Chachnama* as Arabs. Similarly, the early conquerors of northern India were known by their ethnic identity as Turks. After the foundation of their kingdom (AD 1206) they maintained their exclusive ethnic domination and did not share their power and privileges with other Muslim groups. The same policy was followed by other Muslim dynasties. The founder of the Lodhi dynasty, Bahlul (1451-1489), did not trust non-Afghan Muslims and invited Afghans from the mountains (Roh) to support him.

Locally converted Muslims were excluded from high positions and were despised by their foreign (Muslim) brothers. Ziauddin Barani (14th century) cited a number of examples in the *Tarikh-i-Firuzshahi* when the Sultan refused to appoint lower caste Muslims to high posts, despite their intelligence, ability, and integrity. Barani propounds his racist theory by advising Muslim rulers to appoint only racially pure family members to high administrative jobs. He suggested that low caste Muslims should not be allowed to acquire higher education as that would make them arrogant.[1] The theory of racial superiority served to reserve the limited available resources of the kingdom for the benefit of the privileged elite who did not want to share them with others. The ruling dynasties kept available resources in the hands of their own communities and excluded others.

The Mughals wrested power from a Muslim dynasty (AD 1526). On their arrival, therefore, they posed a threat to other Muslim rulers as well as to Hindu rulers. The danger of Mughal hegemony united Muslim Afghans and Hindu Rajputs in a common cause. They fought jointly against Babur in the battle of Khanua (AD 1527). However, Mughal rule changed the social structure of the Muslim community in India, as many Iranians and Turks arrived in India after the opening of the North-West frontier. These new immigrants revived Iranian and Central Asian culture which had been in a process of decline during Afghan rule. To monopolise top positions in the state, Muslims of foreign origin formed a socially and culturally privilged group that not only excluded locally converted Muslims but also Afghans who were deprived of high status jobs. The Mughals were also very conscious of their fair colour, which distinguished them from the converted, darker complexioned Muslims. Since being a Muslim of foreign origin was considered prestigious, most of the locally converted Muslim families began to trace their origin to famous Arab tribes or to prominent Persian families.

The social structure of the Mughal aristocracy changed further when the empire extended its territories and required more people to administer them. Akbar (AD 1556-1605) as the emperor, realised that to rule the country exclusively with the help of Muslims of foreign origin posed a problem as there would not be enough administrators for the entire state. He realised that the administration had to be Indianised. Therefore, he broadened the Muslim aristocracy by including Rajputs in the administration. He eliminated all signs and symbols which differentiated Muslims and Hindus, and made attempts to integrate them as one. Despite Akbar's efforts, however, the rigid social structure did not allow lower class (caste) Hindus and Muslims to move from their lower position in society to a higher status. Class rather than faith was the true dividing line. The Muslim aristocracy preferred to accept upper caste Rajputs as their equals rather than integrate with lower caste Muslims. Akbar's policy was followed by his successors. Even Aurangzeb, in spite of his dislike of Hindus, had to keep them in his administration. He tried to create a semblance of homogeneity in the Muslim community by introducing religious reforms. But all his attempts to create a consciousness of Muslim identity came to nothing. During the entire Sultanate and Mughal periods, politically there was no symbol that could unite the Muslims into a single cohesive community. In the absence of any common economic interest that might bind the different groups of Muslims, they failed to cohere and achieve homogeneity as a single community. *Biradaris*, castes, professions, and class interests kept them politically and culturally divided.

The *ulema* made strenuous attempts to foster a religious consciousness and to build a Muslim identity on such consciousness, by dividing Indian society into believers and non-believers. They fulminated against 'Hindu rituals' being practised mainly by lower-class Muslims and warned them to reform and keep their religion 'pure'. Their attitude towards locally converted Muslims was particularly hostile. They argued that by retaining some of their indigenous Indian customs, they were half Muslims and half Hindus. The *ulema* further argued that true Islam could be understood only through knowledge of Arabic or Persian. Therefore, to integrate with the 'Muslim community' locally converted Muslims should abandon their vernacular culture and learn Arabic and Persian (the everyday language of the ruling elite). By that definition, Muslims of foreign origin were taken to be better than those who had been locally converted. These latter were categorised as ignorant, illiterate, and bad Muslims. However, it must be said that in that period (AD 1206-1707) when the power of the Muslim rulers in India was at its height, no attempts were made to arouse religious, political, or social consciousness on the basis of a Muslim identity. It was only in Akbar's reign, when Rajputs were being integrated with the Mughal nobility, that some *ulema* raised their voice against his religious, political, and social reforms and asserted the separateness of Hindu and Muslim communities. Later on, Aurangzeb tried to rally Muslim support by trying to unite them under a state-imposed version of *fiqh* (Islamic jurisprudence), compiled as the *Fatawa-i-Alamgiri*. But all his efforts failed to arrest the process of political disintegration which he was thus trying to avoid.

During the later period, the decline of Mughal political power dealt a heavy blow to the ruling Mughal aristocracy. Immigrants from Iran and Central Asia stopped coming in due to lack of patronage. The dominance of the Persian language weakened. Urdu emerged as the new language of the Muslim elite. The social as well as the political hegemony of Muslims of foreign origin was reduced. Locally converted Muslims began to claim and raise themselves to a new, higher status.

The rise and successes of the East India Company undermined the role of the Muslim ruling classes. Defeats in the battles of Plassey (AD 1757), Buxar (AD 1764) and, finally, the occupation of Delhi by the British (AD 1803) sealed the fate of Mughal power and threatened the privileged existence of the Muslim ruling elite, as the Mughal emperor became incapable of defending their interests.

Under these circumstances, after Shah Alam II, the practice of reciting the name of the Ottoman Caliph in the *khutba* began. This was meant to indicate that the Ottoman Caliph, and no longer the Mughal emperor, was the defender and protector of the Muslim community in India. Another significant change was that with the eclipse of the political authority of the Mughal emperor, the *ulema* began to represent themselves as the protectors and custodians of the interests of the community. They were now contemptuous of the Mughals whose decline they attributed to their indifference towards religion. They embarked on revivalistic movements which they claimed would lift the community from the low position to which it had fallen. Their revivalism was intended to reform the Muslim community and infuse homogeneity in order to meet the challenges that confronted them.

Sayyid Ahmed's *Jihad* (AD 1831) and Haji Shariatullah's *Faraizi* movements were revivalist and strove to purify Islam of Hindu rituals and customs. Their ultimate goal was to establish an Islamic state in India and to unite Muslims into one community on the basis of religion. Two factors played an important role in reinforcing the creation of a separate identity amongst Indian Muslims. They were, firstly, the activities of Christian missionaries and secondly, the Hindu reformist and revivalist movements. Muslims felt threatened by both. The fear of Muslims being converted into another faith, and of being dominated by others, led the *ulema* to organise themselves 'to save Muslims from extinction'. Recognising the authority of the *ulema*, Muslims turned towards them for guidance. They sought *fatwa* over whether they should learn the English language, serve the East India Company, and regard India as *Dar-ul-Islam* (under which they could live peacefully) rather than as *Dar-ul-Harb* (which imposed upon them an obligation to rebel). Thus, external and internal challenges brought the Muslims of India closer together. Religious consciousness paved the way towards their separate identity. The *madrassa*, mosque, and *khanqah* became symbols of their religious identity. However, the hopes that they placed in religious revivalism as the path to political power came to an end when Sayyid Ahmed was defeated and his *Jihad* movement failed to mobilise Muslims to fight against British rule. Bengali Muslims were subdued with the suppression of the Faraizi movement, and the brutal repression that followed the uprising of 1857 reduced the Muslim upper classes to a shadow of what they had been.

Indian Muslims were demoralised after the failure of the rebellion of 1857. Sadness and gloom prevailed everywhere. Muslims felt crushed and isolated. There came a challenge from British scholars who criticised Islamic institutions as being unsuitable for modern times. Never before had Indian Muslims faced such criticism of their religion. This frightened and angered them. In response, Indian Muslim scholars came forward to defend their religion. This led them to study Islamic history in order to rediscover that they believed to be a golden past. In reply to Western criticism they formulated their arguments, substantiated by historical facts, that Europe owed its progress to the contributions of Muslim scientists and scholars, which were transmitted to it through the University of Cordoba in Moorish Spain, where, under Umayyid rule, there was a policy of religious tolerance towards Christians and Jews. Muslim contributions to art, literature, architecture, and science, thus enriched human civilisation. To popularise this new image of the role of Muslims in history, there followed a host of historical literature, popular as well as scholarly, to satiate the thirst of Muslims for recognition of their achievements. Such images of a golden past provided consolation to a community that felt helpless and folorn. Images of the glories of the Abbasids, the grandeur of the Moors of Spain, and the conquests of the Seljuks healed their wounded pride and helped to restore their self-confidence and pride. Ironically, while glorifying the Islamic past outside India, they ignored the past of the Delhi Sultanate and Mughal India. In their eyes, the distant and outside past was more attractive than the past they had actually inherited. It was left to the nationalist historians of India, mainly Hindu, to reconstruct the glory of Muslim India in building a secular, nationalist ideology in the struggle against British rule.

Muslim search for pride in their Islamic past, thus, once again turned the orientation of Indian Muslims towards the rest of the Muslim world. That consciousness of a greater Muslim identity obscured their Indian identity from their minds. Their sense of solidarity with the Muslim world found expression, especially, in sympathy for the Ottoman empire. Although most educated Indians were quite unaware of the history of the Ottomans, it became a focal point of their pride, displacing the Mughals. Sayyid Ahmad Khan, while explaining the attachment of Muslims to Turkey, said, 'When there were many Muslim kingdoms, we did not feel grief when one of them was destroyed. ... If Turkey is conquered, there will be great grief, for she is the last of the great powers left to Islam.'[2]

During the Balkan wars (AD 1911-1914), when the existence of the Turkish empire was threatened, the sentiments of the Indian Muslims were deeply affected. Muhammad Ali expressed those feelings in these words: 'The Musalman's heart throbs in unison with the Moors of Fez... with the Persians of Tehran... and with the Turks of Stamboul.'[3] The highly emotional articles that appeared in Muslim newspapers such as *al-Hilal*, *Zamindar*, *Hamdard*, *Comrade*, and *Urdu-i-Mualla*, aroused feelings of religious identity. Even secular Muslims turned towards religion, growing beards and observing religious rituals.

The *Khilafat* movement extended the consciousness of a greater Muslim identity amongst Indian Muslims. It also united the *ulema* and Western educated Muslims. The Muslim League, in its session of 1918, invited leading *ulema* to join the party. They grasped the opportunity and soon established control of the movement. When Gandhi supported the Khilafat issue and launched his non-cooperation movement (AD 1919-20), he brought out Hindus to protest in solidarity with the Muslims. But the withdrawal of the non-cooperation movement and the eventual collapse of the Muslims, their unity with the Hindus evaporated.

Support of Pan-Islamism and the Khilafat by the Indian Muslims was the emotional need of the growing Muslim middle class, which was in search of an identity. Rejecting the territorial concept of nationhood, they turned to the Muslim world in order to add weight to their demands. The failure of the Khilafat movement weakened their relationship with the Muslim world and the logic of extra-territorial nationalism came to an end with the end of the Turkish caliphate. The Muslim elite realised that to fulfil their demands they had to assert their separate identity in India. In the words of Prabha Dixit, the Khilafat movement 'constituted an intermediary stage in the transformation of a minority into a nation'.[4]

The assertion of a separate national identity by the Indian Muslims brought them into conflict with the Hindus. The factors that had contributed to distance the two communities were the uneven development of Western education among them, the Urdu-Hindi conflict, the partition of Bengal, the Muslim demand for separate electorates, their demand for quotas for government jobs, and political representation. Communalist feelings in both communities were deepened by revivalist movements of the 1920s. In 1928, in response to the *Shuddhi* (purification) and *Sangathan* (Hindu unity) movements of Hindus, the Muslims formed *Tabligh* (proselytising) and *Tanzim* (organisation) movements to protect Muslim peasants from reconversion to Hinduism. In order to 'purify' the Muslim peasants, Muslim preachers visited distant villages and thus made them conscious of their religious identity. The consequently heightened awareness of their religious identity affected their relationship with the Hindu peasants and communalism greatly damaged their cordial and long-time social and cultural relationship.

This heightened religious consciousness was fully exploited by Muslim politicians when the question of distribution of government jobs and political representation arose. The Muslim elite, in order to get a better share in the name of the Muslim community, made full use of appeals to Muslim identity. Thus, the Two Nation theory arose out of political necessity, and for the first time it highlighted the differences between Muslim and Hindu culture, social life, and history, as well as religion.

Muslim intellectuals provided the theoretical basis of the Two Nation theory by reconstructing Indian history on the basis of religion. Those Muslim conquerors who had long been forgotten and had vanished into the dry pages of history, were resurrected and presented as champions of the Muslims of India. The conquests and achievements of those heroes infused Muslims, high and low, with pride. Ahmad Sirhindi of the 17th century and Shah Waliullah of the 18th, who were not so well known in their own time, were rediscovered by the Muslim elite who searched their writings for legitimation of their theory of two nations in India. Ahmad Sirhindi was the first Indian Muslim 'Alim' who declared that cow slaughter was an important ritual of Islam and should never be abandoned.[5]

There followed an abundance of published literature which was widely read by the Muslim educated classes during this period. The novels of Abdul Halim Sharar, the poems of Hali and Iqbal, and the writings of Muhammad Ali enthralled Indian Muslims and reinforced the consciousness of a distinct Muslim identity. This was essentially on an emotional basis rather than by rational arguments.

The *ulema* also contributed to the infusion of religious feelings amongst ordinary Muslims by organising *milad* festivals and giving a call to go 'Back to the Quran, Back to the Prophet'.[6] They mobilised the common people to take an active part in the religious and political issues concerning the interests of the Muslim community.

The political developments of the 1930s promoted further the consciousness of a Muslim identity. The propaganda of the Muslim League, the success of the Indian National Congress in the 1937 election, and the emergence of Jinnah as the sole spokesman of Indian Muslims, widened the political gulf between the two communities that led ultimately to the partition of the subcontinent.

In the first phase of the history of Muslim rule, the fact that the Muslim elite was in power, kept Muslim religious consciousness dormant. It was invoked only when its grip on power was threatened. For example, Babur appealed to the religious sentiments of Muslim soldiers on the eve of the battle of Khanua but forgot it once the crisis was over. Rather than a religious identity, the Muslim ruling elite asserted an ethnic identity in its bid to hold political and economic privileges. In the second phase, the fall of the Mughals deprived that elite of political power. The task of reviving the sense of their past glory was then left to the *ulema*. The *Jihad* movement of Sayyid Ahmad Shaheed and the *Faraizi* movement of Haji Shariatullah were outwardly religious but aimed at political goals. These leaders, however, sincerely believed that only after the revival of the pure and orthodox faith, could worldly and material success be achieved. Religious piety and political ambitions were interlaced and both provided the incentives to those movements.

In the third phase, the association of the Muslim elite with pan-Islamism was an attempt to derive strength and protection from the Muslim world in order to respond to challenges from the Hindus and the British Government. That movement united Western educated Muslims with the *ulema*. Anti-imperialist sentiments, on the other hand, brought them closer to the Hindus. In their efforts to maintain unity they gave up some of their religious symbols such as cow slaughter. The end of pan-Islamism and the break-up of Hindu-Muslim unity brought about a radical change in Indian Muslim politics. This led to the politicisation of religion.

Thus, in the last phase, consciousness of Muslim identity was exploited by the leadership not so much for a religious cause but for achieving political goals. The leadership was privately secular, but in public they greatly emphasised religion and its values. It is here that the foundations of hypocrisy in appeals to religion were laid, which has persisted to this day. The Partition was regarded as the recognition of the separate identity of the Indian Muslims. But that identity instead of solving their problems has created more crises for the Muslims of Pakistan, India, and Bangladesh.

Notes

1. Ziauddin Barani, *Fatawa-i-Jahandari,* Lahore, 1972.
2. B.R. Nanda, *Gandhi, Pan-Islamism, Imperialism and Nationalism,* Oxford, 1989.
3. *Ibid.,* p. 383.
4. Prabha Dixit, 'Political Objectives of the Khilafat Movement in India', in Mushirul Hasan (ed.), *Communal and Pan-Islamic Trends in Colonial India,* Delhi, 1985.
5. S.M. Akram (ed.), *Darbar-i-Milli,* Lahore, 1966.
6. W.C. Smith, *Modern Islam in India,* Lahore, 1947.

2

Pakistan's Search for Identity

Since its creation in 1947, Pakistan has been in search of a separate identity and legitimacy in order to distinguish itself from India. Compared to India, it was in a disadvantageous position because it adopted a new name which was unfamiliar to most people of the world. Since its creation, it has attached no such glamour and romance to its past civilisation and culture as India. Therefore, to get recognition and place, it had to construct its separate identity. The early leaders of Pakistan fully realised that, by remaining under the shadow of India, Pakistan could not carve its niche in the comity of nations; therefore, they concentrated their efforts on making the new country different from its neighbour. This desire for separateness led to the construction of an Islamic identity, which emphasised the Two Nation theory, the *raison d'etre* for the creation of Pakistan. At the same time, an effort was made to give an exclusive character to the area that comprised Pakistan. To delink this area from the Indian subcontinent, a theory was formulated which propounded that, geographically, the then West Pakistan historically had remained a separate region. Therefore, its present geography justifies not only its creation but also its independence. There was a problem of including East Pakistan in this theory. It was, however, subsequently solved when, in 1971, Bangladesh separated and became an independent country leaving West Pakistan as 'Pakistan'.

From 1947 to 1971, Pakistan went through a number of political crises and experienced military dictatorship and martial law, which changed the role of different power groups such as the bureaucracy, army, and politicians. In the early phase of Pakistan (1947 to 1958), the bureaucracy became very powerful in the absence of an effective political leadership and refused to share its power with any group. After the coup of 1958, the military joined hands with the bureaucracy and ruled the country with an iron hand. However, both institutions, following the colonial heritage, retained some elements of secularism in their outlook and kept the *ulema* out of politics. During Yahya Khan's period, as a result of political turmoil and unrest in East Pakistan, an attempt was made to develop and formulate an ideology for Pakistan. Since then, Pakistan's ideology has been fully supported by the successive civilian and military governments to fulfil their political ends and to legitimise their political power as the defenders of the ideology. In this chapter, an attempt is made to trace the development of Pakistan's ideology as it is understood today.

Construction of the Ideology of Pakistan

The term, 'Pakistan Ideology', was popularised and propagated at a time when Pakistan faced serious political crises after the end of Ayub Khan's rule and East Pakistan's demand for autonomy and an end to the hegemony of West Pakistan. Till then, the term Islamic ideology was used but could not appeal to Bengalis who were mobilised on the basis of linguistic nationalism to get their political rights. Instead, the new term, 'Pakistan Ideology', was used to appeal to the people of both East and West to keep the country united. In the new term, more emphasis was placed on the country (Pakistan) rather than on Islam, because at that time the country, but not Islam, was perceived to be in danger. However, religion remained the basis of the ideology, to be used as a strong bond to keep East and West together. In 1971, Radio Pakistan broadcast the speeches of eleven eminent scholars on the Ideology of Pakistan aiming to 'provide an analysis of the recent happenings in East Pakistan and expose the designs of anti-Pakistan forces, who had been conspiring for long to strike at the very roots of our nationhood'.[1] All the scholars, keeping in view the political situation of East Pakistan, appealed to the people of both wings to remain united on common ideological grounds. Nearly all focussed their remarks within the framework of Muhammad Ali Jinnah's speeches. For example, I.H. Qureshi, quoting Jinnah, remarked:

> The Quaid-i-Azam could have argued that the areas which were to constitute Pakistan had a different history during significantly long periods of time and had characteristics which distinguished them from the other people of the subcontinent. But these arguments never occurred in his mind. The only arguments that he advanced was that the Muslims were different because they were Muslims, not because they were Bengalis or Sindhis, or Punjabis or Pathans, but simply because they were Muslims. And, what in his view made the Muslim different? The basis of the difference was the fact that their entire way of life is founded in the truth, the doctrine and the teaching of Islam.[2]

He also stressed that Pakistan needed an ideology to confront the crises it faced at that time.

> I could say that without ideologies nations can only be dead organism(s). Nations have to cultivate a sense of mission if they want to be truly alive... Indeed, the truth of the matter is that the ideology of Islam should be the guiding force in the life of the country. To the extent that Islam has weakened, Pakistan has weakened. If we possess or want to evolve a common culture, we must not forget that culture can be based only on Islam.[3]

Another writer, Javid Iqbal, explaining the ideology of Pakistan, justifies the domination of the Muslims in Pakistan:

Since Muslims constitute a large majority, they have the right to demand that constitutionally the head of the state of Pakistan must belong to the majority... Similarly, they have the right to demand that the state must promulgate such laws and implement such (an) educational system for their children which (would) promote the moral and spiritual advancement and welfare of its Muslim citizens.[4]

The tragedy of 1971, when Pakistan was dismembered, brought a shock to the people and also a heavy blow to the ideology of Pakistan. Under these circumstances, the argument propounded to save the ideology was that it was misused by the ruling classes and never implemented in its true spirit. According to Sharifal Mujahid:

Islam has been misused not only as a substitutive policy for their low responsive capabilities by various regimes in Pakistan, particularly the Ayub one, but also to justify and sustain status quoism, impose authoritarian or semi-authoritarian rule and even protect vested interests. This exploitation of Islam by the various regimes and the vested interests led to a growing disenchantment with the ideology itself.[5]

Thus, after the debacle of East Pakistan, the new term, Pakistan ideology, besides Islam, covers other aspects which the ruling classes emphasised for the sake of their political domination and to win over people for the cause of a united Pakistan. Now, it has come to mean Islamisation of the state and its institutions, acceptance of the Two Nation theory in South Asia, geographical exclusiveness of the areas of Pakistan, and cultural linkage with Iran and Central Asia.

Process of Islamisation

The process of Islamisation is the outcome of the promises and declarations of the Muslim League leadership to implement the Islamic system in Pakistan. Therefore, after the creation of Pakistan, it was logical to make Pakistan an

Islamic state as it was achieved on the basis of religious nationalism. However, just after its creation, Jinnah, the founder of Pakistan, delivered his first speech in the Constituent Assembly on August 11, in which he declared:

> You are free; you are free to go to your temples, you are free to go to your mosques or to any other place of worship in this state of Pakistan. You may belong to any religion or caste or creed—this has nothing to do with the business of the state (hear, hear)... In the course of time, Hindus would cease to be Hindus and Muslims would cease to be Muslims not in the religious sense, because that is the personal faith of each individual, but in the political sense as citizens of the state.[6]

This speech created problems in the Muslim League leadership as well as in bureaucratic circles because it repudiated the very idea of Pakistan and changed its religious character. Therefore, an attempt was made to censor the speech. Immediately, a press advice was sent to the newspapers not to publish it. Altaf Hussain, the editor of *Dawn*, came forward and threatened the information office that if the order was not withdrawn he would go to Jinnah and tell him the whole truth about it. Only then were the newspapers allowed to publish it.[7] Since then, Jinnah's speech has become a battle-ground between Islamists and secularists. The Islamists and believers in the Pakistan ideology interpret it one way: they argue that the speech was made just to assure the minorities of Pakistan that they were safe in Pakistan. So, it was a message and not a policy statement. 'Moreover, it is unfair to judge his views from (a) single political speech. His other speeches also had to be taken into consideration', writes Manzooruddin Ahmad, after citing a number of quotations from Jinnah's speeches proving that he favoured Pakistan as an Islamic state.[8] So, in the speeches of Jinnah, we find references which suit both the Islamists and secularists. However, as the traditionalists and conservatives have been politically powerful, their version of Jinnah has been promoted, popularised and is now widely accepted in Pakistani society.

After the passing of the Objectives Resolution in 1949, it was argued that the resolution automatically repudiates Jinnah's speech as it provided an Islamic basis to the new country. However, later, additional arguments were given for rejecting this speech. It was said that the speech was just an 'aberration', delivered at a time when Jinnah was very sick. Justice Muneer, writing about this speech says that 'it was described before me as an inspiration by the devil'. Z.A. Bhutto, in a statement to the Supreme Court, observed: 'Under the direction of Information Minister Gen. Sher Ali, attempts were made to have this speech burnt or removed from the records.'[9] During Zia's period, Sharif al Mujahid, the author of Jinnah's official biography and then the Director of the Quaid-i-Azam Academy, gave his interpretation of the speech in which he challenged Jinnah's knowledge of Islam and his competency to pronounce any judgment regarding the Islamic system.

> Though he was fully conversant with the Personal Law in Islam, he was not too acquainted with the Islamic legal system, its ramifications and overall implications. Neither he was well-versed in Islamic lore; nor was he consciously aware of the Islamic implications of various political theories and... historical realities in the evolution of Islam, either in the subcontinent or elsewhere... But to expect him to synthesise the Islamic concept of state with that of the modern Western concept, or to resolve the differences and divergences between them was to ask for the impossible. That was the task of an ideologue and certainly Jinnah was not cut out for that role.[10]

However, the August 11 speech is still used by secularists in support of their position, which puts the conservative elements always on the defensive.

After Jinnah's death, Liaquat Ali Khan, the prime minister, fully supported the efforts to base the new constitution on Islamic principles. The first step towards this goal was taken by the passage in the Constituent Assembly of the Objectives Resolution in 1949, which declares that 'sovereignty over (the) entire universe belongs to God Almighty alone and the authority which He has delegated to the State of Pakistan through its people for being exercised within the limits prescribed by Him is a sacred trust'. The Objectives Resolution was opposed by the Hindu members from East Pakistan. B.K. Dutt referred to the danger of mixing politics with religion and said, 'Politics and religion belong to different regions of mind... Politics belongs to the domain of reason, but you mix it with religion'. As a minority member, he added, 'You (have) condemned us forever to an inferior status'. S.C. Chattopadhyaya, the leader of the Congress, was also very bitter and told the members of the Constituent Assembly: 'You are determined to create a Herrenvolk. ... This resolution in its present form epitomises the spirit of reaction. That spirit will not remain confined to the precincts of this House. It will send its waves to the countryside as well.' For the non-Muslim minorities, he described it as a thick curtain... drawn against all rays of hope, all prospects of an honourable life'. Zafarullah Khan, the foreign minister in Liaquat's cabinent, not anticipating the fate of his Ahmadiyya community in a future Pakistan, defended the Objectives Resolution and assured the non-Muslim minorities that there would be no discrimination against them in the new state.[11]

Liaquat's attempt to make the Objectives Resolution the Preamble of the Constitution, as well as his establishment of the Board of Islamic Teaching *(Talimat-i-Islami)* to advise the Basic Principles Committees on the Islamic aspects of the Constitution, was a deliberate use of Islam to strengthen centralisation and to curb provincialism. However, at this stage, the bureaucracy remained in opposition to the *ulema* and resisted recognising them as the final authority in matters of politics and administration. That is why the proposal to establish the Ministry of Religious Affairs was rejected in order not to give any space to them to play a role in the sphere of administration. However, the *ulema,* in the Constituent Assembly and outside it, mobilised public feelings on the issue of Islamisation. Manzooruddin Ahmed quotes one of them, known as *Muffakir,* who published the 'Draft of Islamic Constitution for Pakistan' (1954), in which he wrote:

> The only basis of Pakistan's nationality is faith in Islam, belief in Allah, resolve to obey the Last Prophet's Shariat and a voluntary contract to associate with the state of Pakistan... Thus, Muslims in Iraq, China, Algeria, may become nationals of Pakistan if they desire so... Pakistan's theory of state is not based on territory, rather it is related to human factors. ... The state, may therefore, extend beyond the frontiers of its main bulk. It is extra-territorial. Potentially the whole universe is under its sway.[12]

After long efforts, the draft of the Constitution was submitted and passed by the Constituent Assembly on Februrary 29, 1956 and came into force on March 23. The Constitution proclaimed Pakistan as the 'Islamic Republic of Pakistan' and the Objectives Resolution as the Preamble of the Constitution. Its significant provisions were that no law repugnant to the Quran and Sunnah should be enacted and only a Muslim could become head of state. The Constitution lasted only 30 months; on the eve of the general election, Ayub Khan, after imposing martial law, abrogated it.

The new Constitution of 1962, which was promulgated by Ayub Khan, despite its secular and modern outlook, contained a number of Islamic provisions which encouraged the process of Islamisation. Initially, the name of the country was proclaimed, 'The Republic of Pakistan'. But, later, as a result of pressure, the term, Islamic was added to it. In the chapter, 'Principles of Policy', it was declared: 'The teaching of the Holy Quran and Islamic ideology to the Muslims of Pakistan should be compulsory'. Further, it said that proper organisation of *zakat*, waqf, and mosques should be ensured. It also introduced the 'Advisory Council of Islamic Ideology' to advise on matters of religion.

The Constitution of 1973 was declared after the defeat of the Pakistan army in 1971 and the independence of Bangladesh. The new constitution also incorporated Islamic provisions in order to win the support of religious parties and groups. Besides, the declaration of the 'sovereignty of God' in the Preamble and the retention of the Islamic name of the state, it declared Islam to be the state religion of Pakistan. It also announced the determination to strengthen bonds with the Muslim world. Further, it required that both the president and the prime minister must be Muslims. In 1974, according to the second amendment, Ahmadiyyas were declared non-Muslims. To further the process of Islamisation, Z.A. Bhutto set up the Ministry of Religious Affairs. To mobilise the religious sentiments of the people, the government expanded the *hajj* policy by terminating the lottery system. The process of Islamisation was further accelerated after the general elections of 1977 in which the opposition launched a countrywide campaign against Bhutto on the charges that he rigged the election. The combined opposition known as the Pakistan National Alliance (PNA) raised the slogan of *Nizam-i-Mustafa* in order to appeal to people's religious emotions. Bhutto, to counter the slogan, announced the implementation of some Islamic laws such as banning drinking and gambling and making Friday a holiday instead of Sunday, and invited Maulana Maudoodi and Maulana Nurani to become members of the Council of Islamic Ideology and cooperate with him in implementation of the Islamic laws. However, his enthusiasm for Islamisation could not keep him in power and, in July 1977, Zia-ul-Haq imposed martial law and ousted Bhutto.

Zia, unlike Ayub Khan, did not abrogate the Constitution, but made a number of amendments which changed the whole shape of it. The Objectives Resolution, which had been so far the Preamble of the Constitution, was incorporated into it and henceforth became a part of it. As Zia required legitimacy, he created his constituency in the circles of *ulema* and *mashaikh* (elders belonging to the families of Sufis). The steps taken by Zia, *zakat* and *ushr* (agriculture tax) laws, *hudood* ordinances (laws of Islamic punishment), setting up a *Shariat* Appeal Bench, interest-free banking known as profit and loss system, *Ahtram-i-Ramazan* ordinance which prohibits eating or drinking openly in public places during the month of fasting, and Pakistan studies and Islamiyat as compulsory subjects on all educational levels.

Zia's policy of Islamisation has greatly affected Pakistan society. The non-Muslim minorities, as a result of separate electorates, are cut off from the mainstream and politically sidelined. Women suffered because of the *hudood* ordinances and *qanoon-i-shahadat* (law of evidence), which downgraded their position and status legally and socially. The Council of Islamic Ideology and the *Shariat* courts empowered the traditional *ulema* who have adopted a very militant and aggressive attitude in demanding further Islamic laws. The establishment of a *majlis-i-shura* in place of an elected parliament created a class of opportunists who were prepared to serve Zia in order to fulfil their political ambitions. The attempt to Islamise education throttled all creativity and research and made the educated class incapable of serving society. It also helped to make them fanatical and reactionary. Not only communalism but sectarianism was the result of some of the Islamic laws, such as *zakat*, which was not accepted by the *Shias*. Further restrictions on Ahmadiyyas disillusioned them, resulting in large-scale migration to Europe and the USA.

The process of Islamisation of Pakistan society did not stop after Zia. Benazir, in her two tenures, kept the situation intact while Nawaz Sharif, following Zia's path, added more Islamic provisions; the Blasphemy Law especially has become a draconian weapon to humiliate or take revenge against the non-Muslim minorities. Nawaz Sharif added the death penalty to the Blasphemy Law, which makes the life of the minorities more miserable and insecure. In his second term, after miserably failing to improve the economy or law and order, he again resorted to using religion and this time announced implementation of the *Shariat-i-Muhammadi* instead of Zia's *Nizam-i-Mustafa*. The Fifteenth Amendment Bill, intended to put the *Shariat* in practice, was passed by the lower house and was waiting to be passed by the Senate, where there was strong opposition to the bill as it would empower the prime minister politically, leaving no chance for the opposition to play any effective role. To counter the opposition to the bill, the prime minister in his speeches asked the *ulema* and the general public to teach a lesson to those who opposed it.

Nawaz Sharif's concept of the *Shariat* was confined only to the Islamic punishment provisions, since he believed that the Islamic penal code would eradicate all crimes from society. Speedy justice and exemplary punishments were viewed by him as the solution to all problems. He was also inspired by *Taliban* Islam in Afghanistan and expressed his desire to imitate it in Pakistan. In January 1999, the provisional government of the North West Frontier Province implemented *shariat* by announcing the *Nizam-i-adl* Regulation in Malakand division, where there is a srong movement of *Tahrik-i-Nifaz-i-Shariat-i-Muhammadi*[13] (TNSM), which is active in demanding Islamic laws. The new law replaced the 1994 Shariat Regulation imposed by the Pakistan People's Party (PPP) government. However, the TNSM leadership is not happy about the *shariat* imposed from above and opposed the mixture of Islamic and Anglo-Saxon laws.[14]

The whole process of Islamisation of the Pakistani Constitution and society shows that Islam has been used by the political leadership repeatedly for political ends. With the failure of the ruling classes to deliver the goods to the people, religion is exploited to cover their corruption and bad governance.

Moreover, the process of Islamisation not only supports but also protects the religious fundamentalists in their attempts to terrorise and harass society in the name of religion. The growing number of *madrassas* (religious schools) and their graduate *taliban* (youth) are becoming a great menace to society. After graduation from the *madrassas*, these people have neither the ability to get a job nor the resources to raise their social status; therefore, finding no place for themselves in society, the best alternative for them is to join a religious party and, after becoming members, work for it. The religious zeal which is inculcated in them is used to crush all un-Islamic practices which, in their view, prevail in society.

In its Februrary 1999 issue, the *Herald* magazine published the activities of such zealous religious youth in Quetta who launched a campaign to implement their type of *Shariat*: 'Armed with batons and moving in large groups, they attacked video rental shops, smashing TV sets and VCRs with impunity'.[15] Similarly, there were reports in the newspapers that, in Malakand division, religious groups threatened to search every house and smash TVs and VCRs, which they consider un-Islamic. The process of Islamisation has created a movement against Western culture and modernity, which are regarded as against the faith of Islam. The result is that Pakistani society, to show its piety, outwardly has become religious. Religious rituals are performed to display religious devotion in order to impress people. Religious writings (Quranic verses or sayings of the Prophet) are displayed publicly on government buildings as well as on private houses. Nearly all Urdu newspapers have weekly religious pages besides publishing religious articles daily.

However, inwardly the society has lost its soul: corruption, moral decadence, social and political degeneration have reached such an extent that everybody has lost any hope to regenerate and revive it.

It appears that, having no vision and alternative, the present and also future ruling classes will continue to rely on the process of Islamisation to preserve their domination. However, in spite of the process, it remains difficult for the religious parties to come to power. The reason is that all major political parties have adopted their agenda and have tried to implement it also whenever they come to power. That is why the religious parties have resorted to violent methods to capture the state through armed struggle. The conflict between the ruling classes and the religious leaders is growing everyday. The religious leaders, since the inception of Pakistan, argue that Pakistan, as an Islamic state, should be ruled by them and not by modern educated leaders because they, and not the political leaders, are the ultimate authority in religious matters. Maulana Maudoodi, the leader of *Jama'at-i-Islami*, despite his opposition to the creation of Pakistan, decided to come to Pakistan in the hope that he would be chosen to lead the new religious state because the Muslim League leadership was not capable of running it according to Islamic tenets. As Pakistan has been declared an Islamic state and Islam the state religion, the *ulema* no longer want to play a secondary role. The political failure of the ruling classes has given them hope that the time is coming when they will be at the helm of affairs like their counterparts in Iran and Afghanistan.

Two Nation Theory

The Two Nation theory is regarded as the cause of the genesis of Pakistan, and, therefore, is an important aspect of the Pakistan ideology. The demand for Pakistan was based on the theory that the Hindus and Muslims were two separate nations with separate cultures and histories and that, therefore, they could not live together. On this assumption, the Indian Muslims demanded a separate homeland where they could observe their religious tenets without fear. These were the political statements made by political leaders such as Iqbal, Jinnah, and Liaquat Ali Khan. To justify it, the Two Nation theory has been provided with a solid historical shape. The task has been accomplished by several historians; among them, the most prominent is I.H. Qureshi, who traces the history of the Muslims in the subcontinent in his book, *The Muslim Community of the Indo-Pakistan Subcontinent*. He argues that the Muslim community maintained its separate identity throughout history. Islam, according to him, was the strong bond that welded different Muslim communities into one. He writes as follows:

> The Muslims of the subcontinent have always been motivated by an intense love of Islam in their policies and movements. ... Their poets have sung more of Islam than of their heroes and achievements; they have preached the ideals of Muslim unity with great fervour, whereas questions relating to their domestic problems have found a secondary place; they have never thought of themselves as an entity separate from the community of Islam.[16]

He further argues that even those Muslims who came from different Muslim countries lost their ethnic identity and, after integrating in the community, identified themselves only as Muslims. 'With the establishment of Muslim rule the same tendency continued. In Sindh, the main centres of Muslim strength continued to become more and more Muslim and less and less Arab, so that gradually the main division came to be between Muslim and Hindu and not between Arab and native'.[17]

Qureshi maintains as a historical fact that the Muslim community in India, even while speaking different languages and living in different regions and absorbing local culture values and traditions, remained separate from the Hindus and rejected all attempts to persuade them to abandon their Islamic identity. Such was the case with Akbar who, after Indianising his empire and incorporating the Hindus in its fold, made an attempt to build an Indian nation. He failed because his policies were challenged by Ahmad Sirhindi (d.1624) who has been resurrected from the past in order to show the historical roots of the Two Nation theory and has become enshrined as its creator and defender. Interestingly, as pointed out by S.M. Ikram, it was Maulana Azad who, in his *Tazkirah*, writes that Ahmad Sirhindi was the lone figure who fought against the atheistic policies of Akbar and thus saved Islam.[18] He was followed by other important religious personalities who kept Islam pure from contamination by Hindu culture, such as Shah Waliullah (d.1762), who made an attempt not only to create unity among different sectarian groups but also to revive the Muslim state even with the help of Ahmad Shah Abdali, the ruler of Afghanistan (d.1772). Then came the reform movement of Haji Shariatullah (d.1840), which followed Sayyid Ahmad's (d.1831), and Ismail Shaheed's (d.1831) *Jihad* movement to purify Islam from Hindu practices, and the failed attempt to set up an Islamic state in the North West Frontier.

Up to this stage, the *ulema* appeared as the protectors and preservers of religious identity and kept the Muslim community intact against all cultural and social onslaughts of the Hindus. In the modern period, however, the situation changed. The *ulema* were relegated to the background while modern educated leaders with a progressive outlook became the champions of the Two Nation theory. At the summit is Sayyid Ahmad Khan (d.1898) who, after the Hindi-Urdu conflict, reached the conclusion that these two nations could not live together. He was followed by Iqbal (d.1938) and finally Jinnah (d.1948), who reiterated the concept of the Two Nation theory and emphasised the separateness of the two communities. The history of the Two-Nation theory comes to an end after partition. There is no further development. Therefore, it has been sometimes said that, after the creation of Pakistan, the Two Nation theory has lost its relevance. Now, a Pakistani nation should be built on the basis of nationalism and the idea of the nation-state. This attempt, however, has been thwarted by the process of Islamisation, which stresses a religious, rather than a secular national identity. This puts the Pakistani people in a dilemma concerning their identity; whether they are first Muslim and then Pakistani or first Pakistani and then Muslim.

Geographical Separateness

As with religious and historical identity, Pakistan also needed geographical identity. Before partition, it was a part of the Indian subcontinent and had no separate identity. In 1947, Pakistan comprised two wings: West and East. So, there was a problem of how to create a geographical identity of these two separate wings. But, after the separation of East Pakistan and the emergence of Bangladesh, the problem of the separate geographical identity of Pakistan became easy to resolve. To have a separate identity it was also essential to delink it from India and assert its separateness and uniqueness. Pakistan's Ahmad Ali, one of the great progressive writers of the pre-partition period, wrote an article which was published in Richard Symonds's book, *Making of Pakistan*, in 1949 as an appendix with the title, 'The Culture of Pakistan'. On the one hand, he claims that the real India is the present Pakistan and, on the other hand, tries to delink this part from the subcontinent. He wrote on this theme as follows:

The word 'India' now adopted as the official name for the new Indian Dominion by the Congress Government, is misleading. If any country, it is Pakistan that could be called by this name. The word 'India' from 'Sind',... which changed to 'Hind' in Iran and the Arab countries and to 'India' in Greece. The most ancient culture to flourish in this subcontinent about four thousand years ago and which, as archaeology proves, was destroyed by the Aryans about 1500 BC had centred round the river Sind or Indus. It was known (to be) akin to Sumerian and Elamite cultures. Even as far back in time as this, it was not 'Indian' in the modern sense of the word. It had more in common with the contemporary civilisation of the valleys of the Nile, Tigris and Euphrates.[19]

He further writes that the Muslims, as inheritors of Greek knowledge and ancient Persian culture, relinked the old contact between this part of the subcontinent and the Middle East and West when they conquered it. 'The valleys of the Tigris and Euphrates, with which the people of Western Pakistan had intercourse as early as four thousand years ago, again began to exercise their influence from the seventh and eighth centuries onwards.'[20]

R.E.M. Wheeler, in his book, also linked the history of present-day Pakistan to the ancient Babylonian and Sumerian civilisations rather than to the Indian.[21] Recently, Aitezaz Ahsan in his book, *The Indus Saga and the Making of Pakistan*, repeats some of these arguments, emphasising the geographical and historical exclusiveness of Pakistan in relation to the Indian subcontinent:

Indus (Pakistan) has a rich and glorious cultural heritage of its own. This is a distinct heritage, of a distinct and separate nation. There is, thus, no fear of any other country devouring or destroying the state. During the last six thousand years, Indus has, indeed, remained independent of and separate from India for almost five and a half thousand years. Only three 'Universal States' those of the Mauryans, the Mughals, and the British, welded these two regions together in a single empire.

He looks at the creation of Pakistan only as a reassertion of that reality: 'It was the reunion of the various units, the Frontier, the Punjab, Sindh, Balochistan, and Kashmir once again in a primordial federation. The mohajirs, who reverted to the Indus in 1947 and thereafter, were the sons and daughters returning to the mother'.[22]

In the 1970s, the independence of Bangladesh and war with India created intense hostility against India. Under these circumstances, attempts were made to delink Pakistan from India and to make it a part of the Muslim world. That was the period when the Middle East, as a result of its oil wealth, attracted people from all over the world. Pakistan took advantage of its Muslim identity to have cordial relations with the oil-rich Arab countries and sent her workers and professionals to earn foreign exchange to boost the weak economy. In order to bring Pakistan closer to the Muslim countries, Z.A. Bhutto hosted the second Islamic summit at Lahore in 1974.

Zia-ul-Haq, during his tenure of 11 years, persistently tried to promote the institution of a Muslim *ummah*. The close relationship with the oil-rich Arab countries, especially Saudi Arabia, helped Pakistan to strengthen its Islamic identity and to make Saudi Arabia a model for its own Islamic system.

The collapse of Russia and the emergence of the Central Asian Republics inspired most of the intellectuals and others in government circles to revive the cultural links with Central Asia. Several articles were published in the newspapers that traced the cultural relationship between Pakistan and Central Asia, claiming that the Pakistani people have a greater affinity with the Central Asian people than with Indians. It was even proposed to make Persian an official language of Pakistan in order to strengthen cultural and political links with Central Asia.

Historical Identity

From its origin, Pakistan has faced problems as to how to reshape the history of the new country. There are three different opinions about the matter. One view is that, since Pakistan came into being in 1947, the history of Pakistan should be started from this point with the understanding that the pre-Partition history would be regarded as the history of India. In the second approach, the history of Pakistan should be written from the Arab invasion of Sindh (711-12 AD) in order to give it an Islamic character. Ancient history before the Arab invasion should be ignored as it is not a part of Islamic history. In the third point of view, it is argued that ancient history cannot be ignored so it should be included in the history of Pakistan. This point of view gives importance to the Indus valley civilisation and provides roots for the territorial rather than religious nationalist interpretation.

The same contradiction occurs in the excavation projects: whether pre-Islamic civilisation should be given importance or more attention should be fixed on the excavations of the Islamic periods. Historical monuments also came under this discussion: which should and should not be preserved? The process of Islamisation and the ideology have changed the approaches to history as well as archaeology.

There is another point of view according to which the history of the Indian subcontinent should be partitioned and history-writing should be confined only to the geographical boundaries of the present Pakistan. During Ayub Khan's period, a *History of Pakistan* was written under the general editorship of I.H. Qureshi; although it was written by the prominent historians of Pakistan, it failed to make any change in the interpretation of history. The most difficult point in writing the history of Pakistan is how to treat the periods of the Salatin and the Mughals. To ignore it means to reject the whole historical period of medieval Indian history when the Muslim rulers ruled over India and contributed to the culture and civilisation of the Indian subcontinent. Keeping in view this problem, this period is given a new name, 'History of Pak-Hind' or History of Indo-Pak. It is also interpreted in terms of Hindu-Muslim conflict. Those rulers who defeated the Hindus, such as Muhammad bin Qasim, Mahmud of Ghazni, and Shihabuddin of Ghaur, are portrayed as heroes and their achievements are glorified and admired. Among the Mughal emperors, Aurangzeb is preferred to Akbar. The emergence of the British as a political power and decline of the Mughals are discussed in a simplistic way as a conspiracy of the Hindus and British against the Muslims.

The modern history of the creation of Pakistan, constructed after the Partition, is given the name, 'Pakistan Movement'. The whole history of the movement is interpreted as having succeeded only because of some great personalities and not because of the people. Since the movement had started from northern India and the Muslim leaders of that area played an important role in making it effective and popular, this would discredit the political leadership of the Punjab and Sindh whose leadership joined the movement only in the end. Therefore, it was not in the interest of the political leadership to give credit to the Muslims of north India; they are simply ignored. Similarly, the Punjab leadership is also not interested in giving the whole credit to Muhammad Ali Jinnah; therefore, Muhammad Iqbal, the poet, is projected as the man who outlined the concept of Pakistan to which Jinnah merely gave practical shape. This helped the Punjab leadership to assert political domination in Pakistan. Now, there is a profusion of literature in which every province highlights its contribution to the struggle for Pakistan. Different social and political groups also claim their contribution to the success of the movement; students, women, *ulema*, journalists and minorities.

The most interesting case is that of the religious parties, especially *Jama'at-i-Islami* which opposed the Pakistan Movement. Now, they are also trying to readjust their position by rewriting or distorting history. One of the books by Maulana Maudoodi, *Musalman aur Mojuda Siyasi Kashmakash* (Muslims and the Present Political Struggle) was rewritten in such a way that all those passages which were against Pakistan and the Muslim League leadership are expunged. Efforts are even made to claim that Maulana Maudoodi is one of the creators of Pakistan. Their interpretation of the Pakistan Movement is that it was for the establishment of an Islamic state and not for political rights or economic benefits.

In an ideological state, efforts are made not only to protect the ideology but also to disseminate it through state agencies, the media, and the school curriculum. Such is the case at least in Pakistan. During his military dictatorship, Zia-ul-Haq coined the phrase, 'geographical and ideological boundaries' of Pakistan, which were the responsibility of his government to defend from external and internal enemies. This declaration made all secular and liberal-minded people enemies of the country. They were warned repeatedly that they would face severe punishment in case of violation of the Ideology of Pakistan. To make the young generation conscious of the Pakistani ideology, the University Grants Commission of Pakistan made Islamic study and Pakistan study compulsory subjects for all students at all levels; even the professional students are required to take the examination in these two subjects besides their professional subjects. The Zia-ul-Haq government also made the two subjects compulsory for 'O' and 'A' level students. The London and Cambridge Boards made them compulsory for Pakistani students. The subject of Pakistan study has given the government the opportunity to teach the students its version of Pakistan's history. Pakistan ideology is described as follows:

> It was a struggle for the establishment of the new Islamic state and for the attainment of independence. It was the outcome of the sincere desire of the Muslims of the subcontinent in which Islam could be accepted as the ideal pattern for the individual's life and also as the law to bind the Muslims into a single community.[23]

Needless to say that both subjects are very unpopular because of their repetitive and hackneyed ideas and lack of any foundations in creative research.

Besides dissemination of the ideology, an additional concern has been to protect it from any criticism and opposition. Article 123(A) of the Pakistan Penal Code, 1860 under the heading, 'Condemnation of the creation of the state and advocacy of abolition of its sovereignty, which was amended in 1992, says:

> [Whosoever] in a manner likely to be prejudicial to the safety [or ideology] of Pakistan, or to endanger the sovereignty of Pakistan in respect of all or any of the territories lying within its borders, shall by words, spoken or written or by sign or visible representation [abuse Pakistan] or condemn the creation of Pakistan by virtue of the partition of India... shall be punished with rigorous imprisonment which may extend to ten years, and shall also be liable to fines.

Conclusion

In asserting her identity, Pakistan is in a dilemma: in case of rejection of the Pakistan ideology, it has to repudiate the very basis of its separation from India; to keep and preserve the ideology means to alienate the non-Muslim minorities from becoming a part of the Pakistani nation. On the other hand, as the ideology has been used by the political and military leadership for their domination by maintaining a high degree of state centralisation it has led to disillusionment in the smaller provinces: they saw in the ideology a tool to snatch their political rights and deprive them of their regional and cultural identities. The alternative suggested by some Pakistani scholars is to reconstruct Pakistani identity on the basis of territorial rather than religious nationalism. Hamza Alavi rightly says: 'By that we will free ourselves from our present-day hang-ups about the so-called Pakistan ideology and its confusing appeal to religion, which only has [the] effect of promoting vicious sectarian conflict'.[24]

Notes

1. M.O. Mohajir, *Ideology of Pakistan,* Radio Pakistan, Karachi, 1971, p. ii.
2. I.H. Qureshi, 'Ideology of Pakistan', in Mohajir, *Ideology of Pakistan,* p. 2.
3. *Ibidi.,* p. 5.
4. Javid Iqbal, 'Ideology of Pakistan', in Mohajir, *Ideology of Pakistan,* pp. 17-8.
5. Sharif al Mujahid, *Ideology of Pakistan,* Sang-i-Meel, Lahore, 1976, p. 23.
6. Quoted in *Report of the Court of Inquiry: Punjab Disturbances of 1953,* Government of Punjab, Lahore, 1954, p. 202.
7. Zamir Niazi, *Press in Chains,* Royal, Karachi, 1986, pp. 34-5.
8. Ahmad Ali, 'The Culture of Pakistan', Note in Richard Symonds, *The Making of Pakistan,* Allied, Karachi, 1966, p. 100.
9. Niazi, *Press in Chains,* p. 36.
10. Sharif al Mujahid, *Jinnah: Studies in Interpretation,* Quaid-i-Azam Academy, Karachi, 1981, pp. 255-56.
11. Symonds, *The Making of Pakistan,* pp. 100-01.
12. Manzooruddin Ahmad, *Pakistan: The Emerging Islamic State,* Allied, Karachi, 1966, p. 97.
13. Movement for the Enforcement of the Shariat of the Prophet Muhammad.
14. *Herald* magazine, Febuary 1999, p. 64.

15. *Ibid.*
16. I.H. Qureshi, 'Muslim Community of the Indo-Pakistan Subcontinent, 610-1947: A Brief Historical Analysis', *Ma'aref*, Karachi, 1977, p. 91.
17. *Ibid.*, p. 93.
18. S.M. Ikram, *Muslim Rule in India and Pakistan,* Students Book Aid, Karachi, 1991, pp. 338, 342.
19. Ali, 'The Culture of Pakistan', p. 197.
20. *Ibid.*, p. 193.
21. R.E.M. Wheeler, *Five Thousand Years of Pakistan,* Royal India and Pakistan Society, London, 1950.
22. Aitezaz Ahsan, *The Indus Saga and the Making of Pakistan,* Oxford University Press, Karachi, p. 8.
23. G.S. Sarwar, *Pakistan Studies,* Tahir, Karachi, 1989, p. 23.
24. Hamza Alavi, *The Territorial Basis of Pakistani Nationhood,* Anjuman Brai Ta'lim, Lahore, 1997, p. 21.

3
New Religious Trends After Partition

I

At the early stage the prophetic religions were guided by divine rulings, but at later stages when divine guidance ceased, religious scholars undertook the task of interpreting the religious texts according to socio-economic and political conditions. As a result, human knowledge made divine guidance subordinate to its interpretation. Every new interpretation claims to be based on the original teachings, but in actuality interpretations keep changing with the requirements of time and give new meaning to scriptures and the sayings of prophets and apostles.

There can be different interpretations of a text and each one contrary to the other because they fulfil the needs of different groups in society. The new meaning of original teachings is never accepted universally, but only by those whose interests it serves. The survival of a religion which has not lost its vitality depends on its being interpreted repeatedly with changing times to re-adjust its teachings to suit different groups, including the ruling classes.

In this chapter an attempt is made to analyse the two antithetical interpretations of Islam which emerged in India and Pakistan after partition keeping in mind the background of their political development. Both interpretations contradict each other but claim to derive their authority from the original teachings of Islam. At the same time, they accuse each other of deviating from the original Islamic teachings and thus betraying the Muslim *Ummah*.

II

The demand for a separate homeland for the Muslims of the Indian subcontinent was to have a country of their own where they could live according to their beliefs. However, the division of India could not solve the problems of the Muslim community. On the contrary, it increased their problems. They are now divided into three parts: Bangladesh, Pakistan and India. The Muslims of India and Pakistan live within two separate political systems. The Indian constitution is secular, but the society contains strong fundamentalist movements which are struggling to convert India into a Hindu state. In the given situation, the question arises as to how the Muslims of India should adjust themselves in the new environment. This new political situation demands a new interpretation of Islam which should ensure that the Muslims are not deviating from Islam by accepting secular and democratic values.

After the decline of the Mughal dynastic rule and the establishment of the British Raj, Sir Sayyid Ahmad Khan (d. 1898) interpreted Islam with a new perspective convincing Indian Muslims to recognise the new realities and adapt themselves to the changes. He adopted a bold approach and rejected the established and prevalent concepts of Islam. He renounced *Jihad*, denied the universality of the institution of the caliphate, and emphasised obedience to the non-Muslim rulers. He argued that serving the British was not un-Islamic because Christians were the people of the book (*Ahl-i-Kitab*) and therefore, there is no religious prohibition to eat with them or to adopt their lifestyle.[1]

Sir Sayyid's interpretation of Islam gave an opening to the Muslim upper classes to come out of their age-old traditions and assimilate a new and progressive culture without having any sense of guilt.

Following the traditions of Sir Sayyid, Muslim intellectuals and religious scholars of modern India are trying to find similarities between Islam and Hinduism to narrow down the differences between the two religions. Of course their task is more difficult than Sayyid Ahmad's because the sanction of friendship and toleration between Islam and Christianity is derived from the Holy Quran and the sayings of the Prophet.

In the case of Hinduism, a broader outlook is adopted arguing that all religions preach peace and love. Some religious authorities, such as Mazhar Jan-i-Jannan (d.1789), are quoted in support as he declares that Hinduism is a divine and prophetic religion, therefore there is no contradiction between the two religions. The main concern of the modern *ulema* and the Muslim intellectuals in India is to remove the past prejudices and prove that the teachings of both religions are based on tolerance. A book edited by Ashfaq Mohammad Khan, *Religion, Muslims and Secularism* in Urdu contains four articles which place emphasis on the common religious and cultural similarities of Islam and Hinduism.[2]

An effort is also made by the new interpretation to reconcile Islam and secularism. In countries where there is a Muslim majority, secularism is regarded as anti-religious and a threat to Islam. On the contrary, in India where the Muslims are in a minority, secularism gives them assurance of their rights and the opportunity to interpret their religion without state control. Therefore, secularism is regarded as essential for the survival of Islam in India.

Maulana Waheedud-din-Khan, an eminent Indian religious scholar, following in the footsteps of Sir Sayyid, makes a bold attempt to reject the classical interpretation of Islam which provides opportunities to the Muslims of India to reconcile and re-adjust themselves in a democratic and secular India. He separates religion and politics, as a combination of the two, in his opinion, would be detrimental to their broader interest.

He writes that in a secular state religions are free to preach and propagate their religions. Thus, Islam in India has an opportunity to set up a *Dawa* empire (*Dawa:* an invitation to accept Islam) and convert people to their religion.[3] He also quotes the opinions of Maulana Saeed Akbarabadi (1908-85) who sees no contradiction between Islam and secularism.[4]

He further argues that for Muslims living in a country where there is no Islamic constitution, the foremost duty is to abide by the rules, regulations and constitution of that country. It is contrary to religious teachings to make any attempt to overthrow the government or be involved in such activities which are detrimental to the system. In non-Muslim countries, the Muslim minority should obey the country's political system. They have two alternatives: either abide by the country's laws or leave the country. The third choice to resist the laws and make an attempt to change them by force, is suicidal for them.[5]

He opposes any attempt to make Islam a revolutionary religion. All movements which follow revolutionary ideals are far from Islamic teachings. Violence becomes a threat to peace and order in a society.[6] Therefore, he argues that the concepts of *jihad* and *Dar-ul-harb* have become obsolete in modern times. He terms such *jihad* movements as reckless, as they damage the cause of Islam. This, in his opinion, is nothing but senseless bloodshed in the name of religion.[7]

He rejects religious nationalism and criticises the movements of Pan-Islamism, the *Khilafat* movement and the *Akhwan al-Muslemeen*. Such movements make the Muslims in non-Muslim countries suspect and erodes their loyalty to their homeland or their adopted country.[8]

He suggests that the Muslims of modern India must understand that the issuance of religious injunctions (*fatwa*) had legality when Islam was a political power and they were implemented by force. Now times have changed. Freedom of expression is allowed in democratic societies. It is against the norms of democracy to burn or censor any publication or prohibit anybody from expressing their opinions. Moreover, it is wrong to think that freedom of expression is a threat to Islam. On the contrary, it allows Islam to propagate its message. So to issue religious injunctions that are contrary to the principles of the freedom of expression is irreligious and an indication of the backwardness of the Muslim mind.[9]

Therefore, there is a general belief among progressive Muslim intellectuals and the enlightened *ulema* of India that the Muslim community should seek democratic and constitutional methods to get its rights rather than adopt the methods of agitation, demonstrations, boycotts which mostly result in violence and clashes with the law enforcing agencies. Maulana Waheed and other Muslim intellectuals are opposed to launching any movement against the government demanding particular rights for Muslims. They argue that the movements which were started by the Muslim League and the Muslim Personal Board resulted in failure and earned nothing but suspicion and hostility against the Muslims. Considering past experience, they are apprehensive of launching any movement in the name of religion because it would unleash the forces of communalism against Muslims.

Like Sir Sayyid Ahmad Khan, whose interpretation suited the rising European educated Muslim class of his time, the present interpretation is in the interest of the educated Muslim middle class, which is eager to keep its Muslim identity and to join the mainstream of Indian society. As far as the ordinary Muslims are concerned, they are still pawns in the hands of the orthodoxy.

III

As far as Pakistan is concerned, in the first phase of its history, the government of Liaquat Ali Khan invited the leading *ulema* to help in drafting the Constitution according to Islamic principles. They were successful in drafting the 'Objectives Resolution' which later became the preamble of the Constitution of 1956. The martial law of 1958 dashed all hopes to make an Islamic constitution or to establish an Islamic state in Pakistan. In the 1970 general elections, the religious parties appealed to the electorate to vote for them in order to concretise the dream of converting Pakistan into an Islamic state.

However, the results were disappointing for the religious parties as they failed to win sufficient seats in the National Assembly (Jamaat-i-Islami won only four seats). In 1985, under Zia-ul-Haq there were partyless elections, the results of which were also not in favour of the religious parties. In 1988 and 1990, the Jamaat-i-Islami contested the election along with other political parties, but its programme in the election did not impress its allies and in 1990 they, in spite of the victory of its ally, Nawaz Sharif, could not allow it to play an effective role in the government.

In 1993, the Jamaat-i-Islami contested the election in its independent capacity and appealed to the people to elect it as a third alternative, but again it failed. In 1997, the Jamaat had no option but to boycott the elections. The successive failures in the elections convinced the Jamaat that democracy is ill-suited to Islam. Other parties, such as the Jamiat-i-Ulema-i-Pakistan, announced that they would not take part in the elections after their defeat in 1990 and 1993. This also applies to the Jamiat-i-Ulema-i-Islam.

Maulana Tahir-ul-Qadri, a religious scholar, founded the Pakistan Awami Tehreek in 1989. He took part in the elections of 1990 and 1993 in which his party failed to get any seat. After that he also announced that his decision to contest the election was a test to see whether there was any possibility to come to power by democratic means and implement the *Shariat*. But the experience led him to the conclusion that it was not the right method to achieve the Islamic revolution. Therefore, he renounced the traditional and democratic politics and turned towards revolutionary politics.[10]

Hence in Pakistan the attitudes of the *ulema* and the policies of the religious parties are anti-democratic and anti-secular. From the very beginning, the term secularism is considered anti-Islamic in religious circles. It is translated into Urdu as *La Diniyat* (absence of religion), meaning that not only the state but society is also not allowed to have any religion. Hence, secularism becomes a threat to the existence of Islam.

Javaid Akbar Ansari, an ideologue of Jamaat-i-Islami wrote an article in Urdu entitled 'The Action Programme of Jamat-e-Islami and the other Religious Parties' with the subheading 'The destiny of the *ulema* can only be changed by Jihad'. He presents an outline of how religious parties should launch a campaign against secularism. In the first place, they should accuse the secular political parties of causing the present political crisis in the country and convince the people that their grievances are the result of the secular system. Both secularism and democracy, in his opinion, mislead people by mobilising them to get their socio-economic and political rights.

Once people expect to gain more rights, they deviate from the religious path. Thus, the struggle against secularism and democracy is the struggle against the demand of rights by the people. He argues that if the religious parties are involved in the politics of rights then they have to think of the demands of the people rather than implementation of religious teachings. The aim of the religious parties should be to implement the *Shariah* and not to fight for people's rights. Therefore, the correct policy is that all religious parties should renounce traditional politics and adopt the politics of *jihad*.[11]

Another writer, Abdul Wahab Suri, in an article 'Democracy: A Tragedy of the Islamic Movements' condemns democracy because it fails to determine the status of an individual on the basis of his ideas. A drunkard and a pious man both have equal rights and status in a democratic society, both have a right to vote and a right to express themselves. In a democracy, rights are more important than virtue and piety. Therefore, he also argues that if religious parties become a part of this democratic process they would lose their Islamic character.[12]

Both Islamic intellectuals are against liberalism and a liberal constitution because they believe that a free and liberal environment is un-Islamic and detrimental to religious values.[13]

Ansari's concept of *jihad* is very broad. It includes a struggle against all irreligious activities prevalent in society. He urges that a campaign against the population department and the Women's Division of the Government of Pakistan should be launched because both departments affect Islamic family values by granting rights to women. He argues that the Aga Khan Foundation should also be forced to close down and all women's NGOs should be banned. Five star hotels and clubs should be targeted as they promote un-Islamic activities and encourage their customers to celebrate the new year and other un-Islamic festivals. If there are merry-making parties in the affluent areas such as Defence or Clifton in Karachi, Gulberg in Lahore and Sector 'F' in Islamabad, these should be disturbed by the armed groups of the Islamic parties.[14]

IV

The Afghan *jihad* against the occupation forces of Russia gave an impetus to the religious parties to play active roles in politics. The American and Western funding and supply of sophisticated weapons made the *Mujahideen* a powerful force. The coming of volunteers from Saudi Arabia, Sudan, Egypt, Algeria, and various other Muslim countries, gave an international outlook to the *jihad*. When the Russians left Afghanistan, the credit was taken by the *Mujahideen*. It encouraged them to fight a holy war against all enemies of Islam. As the Jamaat-i-Islami played an active role during the Afghan crisis, it is believed to have amassed huge amounts of wealth. Consequently, the Jamaat-i-Islami changed its policy and raised the slogan of the Islamic revolution.

Javaid Ansari theorises the Jamaat-i-Islami's policy of *jihad* by saying that it is a continuation of the *jihad* movement started by Imdadullah Makki in 1858 during the War of Independence. Later the Deoband school and its leaders deviated from this policy and turned towards constitutional methods. Consequently the *Jihad* movement lost its popularity. That is why during the freedom struggle against British colonialism, the Muslim community either supported the Congress or the Muslim League.[15]

Ansari argues that Maudoodi's first book called *Al-Jihad* indicates that in order to achieve political ends priority should be given to *jihad*. Maudoodi believes that in a secular system, Islam cannot become a dominant religion, but in a liberal and democratic society, an Islamic system can be maintained. Ansari refutes Maudoodi and says that fifty years of democracy in Pakistan have proved him wrong. In his view it is not possible to establish an Islamic system in a liberal and democratic set up. With the strength of a democratic system, Islamic traditions and values become weak.[16]

However, it is beyond the capacity of the Jamaat-i-Islami to follow the policy of *jihad* as the majority of its followers belong to the middle classes whose interest is to have a secure and peaceful life. The main concern of this class is to get its children educated and have a successful career. They want peace, security and protection in their old age. Their financial condition does not allow them to engage in *jihad* activities. However only a bunch of young people joined the *mujahideen* trained by the Jamaat-i-Islam to fight against the enemies of Islam.

Keeping in view past experience, Ansari outlines the structure and agenda of the future Islamic state. He says that militarily it should be strong and able to fight against US influence. It should have the capacity to fight against India till the problem of Kashmir is settled. The Islamic state should have a strong centre and a firm policy to eliminate the opposition.[17]

He argues that a society cannot be changed by sermons or preaching. This has been proven by the ineffective preaching of the Tablighi Jamaat. Therefore, *jihad* is the only alternative. He hopes that Muslims living in America and European countries would attack the enemy from within; if the imperialist powers attack any Islamic country, the Muslim community would counter attack them in New York and London.[18]

In practical terms, it is doubtful whether the Jamaat-i-Islami would launch an armed struggle to topple the state. The policy of the Jamaat-i-Islami is changing radically. Recently, it has opened its membership to all Muslims. Previously it was restricted only to men of piety. They have put up sign boards throughout the country to invite people to join the Jamaat-i-Islami in fighting against corruption and backruptcy of the political leadership.

This shows that the Jamaat-i-Islami does not want to overthrow the state by armed struggle but use street power and adopt methods of agitation, demonstrations, 'gherao/ dharna' and by organising rallies, public meetings and through effective propaganda and human struggle, overthrow the government. But, even if successful, the question is how to come to power without popular support and without winning the election? The answer to this question is not to be found in the policies of Jamaat-i-Islami.

V

Dr. Asrar, a renegade from the Jamaat-i-Islami, is the *ameer* of the Tanzeem-e-Islami which he declares to be the Islamic revolutionary organisation. His concept of leadership differs from other religious parties. He believes that an Ameer of an Islamic movement or organisation should not be elected by the members of the party. Instead, anyone who feels confident and competent should invite people to follow him. The leadership from above would liberate him from the obligation of voters and allow him to implement the Islamic programme without having any pressure from below.[19]

Following this concept, Dr. Asrar, as an *ameer*, demands from his followers an unconditional obedience and complete subordination. Besides the Tanzeem-e-Islami, he also launched the *Tehreek-i-Khilafat* whose aim is to revive the classical system of *khilafat* to counter Western democracy.[20]

Both Tahir-ul-Qadri and Dr. Asrar are careful to talk about *jihad* as an armed struggle. In their view, the concept of Islamic revolution is character building and not a bloody revolution.

Since the followers of these two *ulema* come from the business class and from among retired government officers, it is not in their interest to get involved in any armed struggle. Their main concern is to preserve what they have so far accumulated. By supporting these two religious parties financially, they not only legitimise their black money, but also earn respect in society. Thus the programme of character building and religious training suits them as it does not challenge the status quo and leaves their property intact.

VI

The ambivalent policy towards *jihad* left a vacuum for an extremist religious group to fill it. In 1986 a new organisation, Markaz-al-Dawa wal Irshad emerged at a time when the Afghanistan war was at its peak. The organisation actively participated in the Afghan *jihad*. In 1990, it set up a military camp in the Afghan province of Kunhar where not only Pakistanis, but also those from the Philippines, Somalia, Sudan, Bosnia, Macedonia, USA, England and Arab countries came for training. The *Lashkar* or the army which is trained by the organisation is known as *'Lashkar-i-Tayyiba'* (the army of the Puritans).

In Pakistan, the Dawa-al-Irshad set up their training centre at Murid Kay near Lahore, where the Talibans are not only militarily trained but also get religious education. It is compulsory for all students to keep beards, dress according to Islamic morality and strictly follow Islamic teachings. They are not allowed to watch TV or listen to the radio or music. All newspapers, before going to the reading room, are censored, and pictures are especially torn away from newspapers and magazines. The organisation proudly claims that its *Mujahideen* fought in Bosnia, Kashmir, Afghanistan, Algeria, Chechnya and the Philippines.

The Markaz completely rejects the traditional politics of agitation, demonstrations, strikes or pressurising the government by passing resolutions. For them the policy of blood and iron is the only solution to all problems. However, at this stage it is not their policy to confront the Pakistani government. On the contrary, their policy is to fight outside

Pakistan.[21] Pakistan is used as a base for training the *Mujahadeen*. It is a well-known fact that the organisation is getting support from Saudi Arabia and, perhaps, also from local sources.

Besides al-Irshad there are twenty or twenty-two lashkars of different religious groups. Prominent among them are Hizb-al-Mujahadeen, Sipah-i-Sahaba, Sipah-i-Mahammadi, Jammaat-al-Mujahadeen-i-Pakistan, Harkat al-Ansar Pakistan, Sipah-i-Khalid, Al Mukhtar force, Al Abbas force, Jhangvi force and Ahl-i-Hadis force. Most of these forces are funded by Middle Eastern countries.

Unlike the Jamaat-i-Islami and the Tanzim-i-Islami, their supporters belong to the lower classes, those who do not have any social status in society. They are financially weak and educationally backward. Their association with these armed groups in the name of *jihad* inspires them to join and sacrifice their lives for the cause of religion. Moreover, the association also gives them an identity, a status, social support and a purpose in life.

The *madaris* (religious schools) are the breeding grounds where religious zealots, belonging to different Islamic sects, are organised and trained to fight against the enemies of Islam. These Taliban belong to the poor and lower classes of the society which cannot afford to join private or government schools. The *madaris* not only admit them but provide them free lodging and boarding. However, there is no assured career for the Talibans, except to become religious teachers or imams of mosques. Thus every sect has its own mosque which is a source of income for imams, muazzins and religious teachers.

There is, furthermore, a sectarian war between the Shias and Sunnis which is fought by the Sipah-i-Sahaba and Sipah-i-Mohammadi. It is a well-known fact that they are funded by Saudi Arabia and Iran respectively.

The armed religious groups, however, do not have any popular support. Therefore, when they fail to obtain funds they rob banks, commit dacoity and force shopkeepers to pay them protection tax. As a result of it, they are despised by the people.

VII

The decision of the religious parties and groups to abandon democratic means, and adopt the policy of revolution or *jihad*, is not helping them to get popular support. Instead they are losing credibility. The Taliban phenomenon in Afghanistan is inspiring them to play the same role in Pakistan. But the social attitude of Pakistanis is different. In Pakistani society, a *maulvi* does not have a very respectable position. In the Punjab, he is regarded as a *kammi* (ordinary worker), who depends on a public role. In spite of getting foreign funds and becoming financially strong, he fails to raise his social status. In the rural areas, leadership is in the hands of the feudals who also safely win elections from their constituencies. Thus the religious parties hardly have any place in the rural areas. Most of these parties are urban-based and have some support from the middle classes. Even this support eroded when the nationalist and linguistic parties emerged in Sindh and Balochistan.

Moreover, the people of Pakistan are not prepared to accept religious rigidity, especially in the rural areas. Their concept of religion is tolerance and coexistence with other religions. They do not have any place for puritanism or extremism in their lives. It is sad that no religious party represents the general will of the people. So far people have refused to be a part of the religious wars conducted by these groups. There is no sectarian riot or conflict from below; they are always from above.

In India, new religious interpretation is trying to make Islam relevant to democracy and secularism. There is an effort to make Islam a religion of peace and tolerance. In Pakistan, on the contrary, politics is an inseparable part of religion. Therefore, all religious parties, except one or two, aspire to seize political power and convert the country to an Islamic state according to their beliefs. This makes Islam a tool in the hands of religious parties to achieve their political ends. There is also an effort to force people to abandon tolerance and accept the extremist religious views. Sectarian riots are leading common people in the direction of violence. There is also another difference between Indian and Pakistani Islam. In India, religious scholars, free from state control, are discovering different aspects of Islam, while in Pakistan there is more emphasis on physical force rather than intellectual discourse. This is evident from the writings of the *ulema* of both countries. Continuing the 19th century trends started by Sir Sayyid, Indian religious scholars are debating how to reconstruct religion on the basis of new socio-economic and political changes; while in Pakistan, there is no attempt to understand the demands of the modern period and to adjust Islam accordingly. Old solutions are offered to new problems.

The Pakistani religious parties are apprehensive that the new Indian interpretation of Islam might influence the Muslims of Pakistan. So they are forcefully refuting and condemning it. However, there is a section of society which is avidly reading the new material on Islam written by Indian scholars. If the Indian version of Islam, which believes in the separation of politics, secularism, democracy and tolerance, has any impact in future, Pakistani political development may change its course.

Notes

1. Sir Sayyid, *Khutbat I,* Lahore, 1972, pp. 224-25; *Maktubat,* Lahore, 1959, p. 188; *Maqalat II*, Lahore, 1961, p. 51; *Maqalat IX*, Lahore, 1962, pp. 19-20. For more details see Altaf H. Hali, *Hiyat-i-Jawaid,* Lahore, 1946, pp. 62-4, 332, 467.

2. For details see Ashfaq M. Khan, *Mazhab, Mussalman and Secularism,* Lahore, 1946. The articles are Akhlaq Hussain Dehlawi, 'Vedic Dharam and Islam: A Comparative Study', pp. 21-32; Shaheen Jamal, Shri Ram, Ramayain, *Mussalman and the Holy Prophet,* pp. 33-8; Nisar Ahmad Faruqi, *Our Composite Culture and Mysticism,* pp. 39-46; Khwaja Hasan Sani Nizami, *Sufism and Hindu Mysticism,* pp. 53-62.
3. Waheed-ud-din Khan, *Fikr-i-Islami,* Lahore, 1996, pp. 28-87.
4. *Ibid.*, p. 105.
5. *Ibid.*, pp. 143-44, 158.
6. *Ibid.*, p. 82.
7. *Ibid.*, pp. 84, 143-44, 153-54, 155-58.
8. *Ibid.*, p. 18.
9. *Ibid.*, pp. 58-66.
10. Tahir-ul-Qadri, *Tahrik-i-Minhaj ul Quran,* Lahore, 1996, pp. 99-100.
11. Javaid A. Ansari, 'Future Guidance for Jamat-e-Islami and Other Religious Parties' (Urdu) in Monthly, *Sahil,* Karachi, No. 4, February 1997, pp. 51-5.
12. A. Suri, 'Democracy: A Tragedy of the Islamic Movements', in Monthly, *Sahil,* Karachi, No. 4, February 1997, p. 70.
13. A. Suri, *op. cit.*, p. 70; Javaid A. Ansari, *op. cit.*, p. 59.
14. Javaid A. Ansari, *op. cit.*, p. 59 (in 1992 Islami Jamiat-i-Talaba, a student of the Jamaat-i-Islami attacked the house of Collin David, a Lahore-based artist, and disturbed his exhibition. In 1993, the group of the same organisation smashed the cars outside the Punjab Club on New Year's Eve.)
15. *Ibid.*, p. 50.
16. *Ibid.*, p. 51.
17. *Ibid.*, p. 58.
18. Javaid A. Ansari, Criticism on Waheed-ud-din Khan's book *Fikr-i-Islami* (Urdu) Monthly *Sahil,* Karachi, No. 4, April 1997, p. 40.
19. *Tanzim-i-Islami,* Lahore (n.d), p. 7.
20. *Pakistan main Nizam-i-Khilafat* (System of the Khilafat in Pakistan), Lahore (n.d), p. 5.
21. Introduction to *Mujahadeen Lashkar Tayyiba* (a pamphlet published by the Markaz), Lahore (n.d).

4

History, Ideology and Curriculum

To control the past is to master the present, to legitimise dominion and justify legal claim. It is the dominant powers—or finance the media or means of production, whether it be school books or strip cartoons, films, or television programmes.[1]

In the past, rulers and aristocrats used history to glorify their achievements as saviours and benefactors. In the modern period, political leaders use it to assert their authority and domination and legitimise their status as rulers. In the newly independent countries, particularly, leaders reconstruct history to suit their agenda in the changing political situation.

After decolonisation, a new generation of political leaders, who had struggled for freedom and assumed the status of freedom fighters, claimed to rule the newly independent countries. As rulers they were in need to legitimise their claims. This is why the concepts of the 'freedom struggle' and 'war of liberation' emerged with great lustre and romance. Sacrifices of these leaders have become dominant themes in recent history writing. In India and Pakistan, the role of these freedom fighters is highly eulogised in order to give them the right to rule the new nations. Interestingly, British historians describe the freedom struggle as a 'transfer of power', implying that the change that took place was a voluntary surrender of power and not as a result of struggle. These two interpretations reflect two antithetical approaches to history.

Like most of the newly independent countries, Pakistan also had problems about how to reconstruct its history in order to legitimise its creation. It faced two problems: how to treat the colonial period, and how to justify partition. Most of the colonised countries have been sensitive about their colonial periods, which marked their humiliation, surrender and defeat. Dealing with these periods requires an acceptance of national and societal weakneses in these countries. Pakistan found an easy solution. It looked at the whole period of colonisation as the Indian past because Pakistan had not existed at that time. It left it to the Indian historians to deal with the colonial period. However, the Pakistani historians had to grapple with several complicated and complex issues on the partition of India. While handling these, they kept in mind the interests of the ruling classes.

In Pakistan, historiography has developed under the framework of the 'Pakistan Ideology', which is based on the idea of a separate Muslim nationhood and justifies the partition of India. The Pakistani historians are told from the very beginning to construct their history within this framework. It is well understood that whenever history is written under the influence of an ideology, its obejectivity is sacrificed. Facts are manipulated in order to justify the political acts of leadership. Eric Hobsbawm has said: 'Nationalist historians have—often been—servants of ideologists'.[2] He observed: 'History as inspiration and ideology has a built-in tendency to become a self-justifying myth. Nothing is a more dangerous blindfold than this, as the history of modern nations and nationalism demonstrates'.[3]

In power politics, an ideologically based historiography provides legitimacy to the political leadership. Michael W. Apple poses the question: What does ideology do for the people who have it? He writes that it 'distorts one's picture of social reality and serves the interest of the dominant classes in the society'.[4]

Pakistani historians also face the problem of how to deal with the ancient past. Islam came to the Indian subcontinent in the 8th century. On the basis of the Two-Nation theory, the ancient Indian past does not belong to the new country. A teacher and a Jamaat-i-Islami member, Asadullah Bhutto, once gave a press statement that Mohenjo Daro and other such archaeological remains should be bulldozed as they do not belong to Islam. Turning their attention to the early Islamic past, the historians seek an Islamic link with the Arab conquest of Sindh, known in history textbooks as 'the door of Islam' (*bab ul-Islam*). According to them, the conquest of Sindh made the Indian Muslims a part of the Arab empire. This makes them more enchanted with the glories of Damascus, Baghdad, Cairo, and Cordoba than with the Indian counterparts of Delhi, Agra or Fathepur Sikri. They also trace Central Asian links. A reputed Pakistani archaeologist and historian, A.H. Dani, has said that Pakistan has closer and stronger cultural links with Central Asia than with India.

How one treats medieval Indian history is also problematic. During this period, Muslim dynasties ruled over India but the centre of power was situated in India and not in the area that constituted the new country of Pakistan. Though the period is reconstructed under the title of 'History of Pak-Hind', there are some fundamentalists who totally reject the rule of the Muslim dynasties as being un-Islamic on the grounds that the Muslim rulers preferred to rule on the basis of secularism and did not establish an Islamic state. They inducted the Hindus in their administration and weakened the Islamic character of the state. These historians also condemn all attempts that led to the development of a composite culture. I.H. Qureshi, a leading historian, criticised the policy of cooperation with Hindus that was enunciated by Mughal rulers, especially Akbar, who included Hindus as partners and treated them equally.

Qureshi has argued: 'And in the final analysis, if the Muslims were to forget their uniqueness and come to absorb as Akbar did, contradictory tendencies and beliefs from other religions, could the Muslim nation continue to exist as a separate nation? Akbar's policies created danger not only for the Muslim empire but also for the continued existence of the Muslim nation in the subcontinent'.[5] Akbar is much maligned in Pakistani historiography and is completely omitted from the school textbooks.[6]

Recently in an article entitled 'At Last the Fall Became Our Destiny', a Jamaat-i-Islami intellectual wrote: 'After Muhammad bin Qasim, all conquerors invaded India for plunder and not for (the) propagation of Islam. They had no desire and passion for holy war. Some of them conquered territories after shedding Muslim blood and assumed the royalty that was similar to the Romans and the Persian rulers'.[7] He condemned them for emulating the practices of the non-Muslim kings: 'They built palaces and castles for their luxurious living and personal protection, kept slave girls for their sexual satisfaction, and recruited eunuchs to watch the conduct of their women. Following the traditions of the Pharaohs, they even built tombs for their queens'.[8]

He said that the reason for the downfall of the Muslim rule in India was the attempt to create a composite culture. When Akbar and other Mughal rulers adopted the policy of marying Hindu women, the process of polluting Muslim culture began, which ultimately led to the disintegration of the Mughal empire. He wrote: 'When the Mughal rulers married Hindu women and allowed them to keep their religion and worship according to their religion, it was disaster. As a result of these marriages, Mughal rulers were born from Hindu mothers'.[9] Medieval Indian history is not regarded as a part of Pakistani historiography because the Hindus and the Muslims both shared it. The culture that was produced by both is looked upon as a denial of Muslim separateness.

Problems Posed by Recent History

In dealing with the recent history of the freedom struggle, the emphasis has shifted from the freedom struggle to the 'struggle for Pakistan'. The Congress, dominated by Hindus, is considered to be the main adversary because it did not recognise the Muslim community as a separate one and opposed partition. This approach makes the Hindus more hostile to the Muslims, than the British. Therefore, the creation of Pakistan is regarded as a victory against the Hindus and not against the British.

The reconstruction of the regional histories poses another problem. How does one adjust them in the ideological framework? In the case of Punjab, its Sikh period is rejected and downgraded as the 'Sikha Shahi', which is synonymous with anarchy and disorder. The wars of the Sikhs, which were fought against the British, have no place in history textbooks. On the other hand, the British conquest of Punjab is hailed as a blessing for the people of Punjab because it delivered them from Sikh rule.

The British ignominiously defeated the Talpur Mirs, the rulers of Sindh, in 1843. To minimise the humiliation of the defeat, historians attempt to glorify some individuals who fought bravely against the British. Sindh is given credit because its legislative assembly was the first to vote for joining Pakistan. The North West Frontier Province is remembered for its resistance to colonial rule but the allegiance of its political leadership to the Congress is condemned. The political leadership and not the people are blamed. On Balochistan, the resistance of the Kalat state not to accede to Pakistan is not mentioned in the school books.

Pakistani historiography tries to homogenise the culture, traditions, and social and religious life of the people. This suits the political attempts towards centralisation. Any attempt to assert the historical identity of a region is discouraged and condemned. This also affects the non-Muslim religious minorities, who are also excluded from the mainstream of history.

Pakistan has passed through many political crises. It has experienced military dictatorships, the corruption of feudal democracy, the separation of East Pakistan, the rise of fundamentalism and ups and downs in relations with India. History textbooks became the victim. History as a subject was discontinued in 1961 and was incorporated into the textbooks on social science.

Textbook writers are allowed to select only those portions of history, which suit the ruling party in power. Michael W. Apple observes: 'Selectivity is the point; the way in which from a whole possible area of past and present, certain meanings and practices are chosen for emphasis, certain other meanings and practices are neglected and excluded. Even more crucially, some of these meanings are reinterpreted, diluted, or put into forms which support or at least do not contradict other elements within the effective dominant culture'.[10]

When there is democracy, army rule is blamed for all existing problems; when the army comes to power, it accuses politicians and democracy for causing disorder and corruption. Even when there is a democratic change, the past government is condemned for political and economic problems. As George Orwell said: 'All history is scraped clean and reinscribed, exactly as often as is necessary. The past is written in the light of the present requirements of the authoritarian government'.[11]

The disjointed and selected version of history fails to create any historical consciousness among students and the general public. When full facts of historical processes are not recorded, it reduces the power of analysis and society is condemned to repeat its history over and over again.

Notes

1. Marc Ferro, *The Use and Abuse of History*, Routledge and Kegan Paul, London, 1984, p. vii.
2. Eric Hobsbawm, *On History*, Abacus, London, 1999, p. 35.
3. *Ibid.*, p. 47.
4. Michael W. Apple, *Ideology and Curriculum*, Routledge and Kegan Paul, London, 1980, pp. 20-21.
5. I.H. Qureshi, *The Muslim Community of the Indo-Pakistan Subcontinent*, 1962, p. 167.
6. Mubarak Ali, *History on Trial*, Lahore, 1999, pp. 76-82.
7. Zahid Ali Wasti, 'And the Fall became a Destiny' (Urdu article) in *Awaz*, No 9, October-December 1999, pp. 247-48.
8. *Ibid.*, p. 248.
9. *Ibid.*, pp. 250-7.
10. Michael W. Apple, *op. cit.*, p. 6.
11. George Orwell, *Selected Writings*, Heinemann Educational Books, London 1976, p. 165.

5

Development of the Discipline of History in Pakistan[1]

Introduction

When we discuss the state of history as a subject in our educational institutions, people raise a number of questions: what is the use of history in the technological age? How far is it relevant to our present problems? And if it fails to create any political and social consciousness in society then what is the use of studying it? Some people even go further and raise quite a different set of questions: is it a market-oriented subject? If not, then why should students waste their time and money to study it? These are valid questions, especially at a time when there is unemployment and every young person wants to have a successful career. These questions are also valid because our historians have failed to correct the falsification and distortion of colonial history, and did not offer any effective response to modern challenges. The study of history has neither been constructed objectively, nor has the history of the world and civilisation of humankind been studied with an open mind.

Not a single history department in any university has specialised in any particular aspect of history. Our higher educational institutions do not provide any new interpretation that could lead to the formation of historical ideas and philosophy. If we analyse the discipline of history in the light of the above questions, we reach the conclusion that the history that we teach in our schools, colleges and universities is distorted to the point of being deformed. Those who are responsible for the history curriculum are not aware that the subject has changed drastically over the last several decades. It no longer remains confined to politics, but has broadened itself to involve the social and cultural aspects of society. There are different schools of historical studies that have enriched the subject, such as 'History from below' or the approach of the 'Annals School' to construct the history of sensibilities. If the subject is taught in such a broad perspective, only then can it be useful to society.[2]

State Ideology and History

Our state uses the subject for its own political and ideological interests. It is claimed that Pakistan came into being as a result of an ideological struggle. Therefore, the official purpose of history in Pakistan is to legitimise the state's ideology and write history within a framework that suits the ruling classes. This is manifested especially in history textbooks, in which selective information is imparted to students with an underlying motive to make them chauvinistic, nationalist and religiously conservative. M. Ikram Rabbani, in his textbook, which is prescribed in English medium schools, writes about the ideology of Pakistan:

> Pakistan ideology is based on the fact that the Muslims are a separate nation, having their own culture, civilisation, customs, literature, religion and way of life. They cannot be merged in any other nation because their philosophy is based on the principles of Islam. As the Muslims of India found it extremely difficult to live according to the Islamic principles of life in the United India, they were forced to demand a separate homeland to safeguard their national and religious identity.[3]

Because of ideological considerations, the subject has suffered immensely. To date, no decision has been taken as to how to treat the ancient past. Should we ignore ancient history because it is pre-Islamic? How do we deal with the medieval period. When the Muslim dynasties ruled over India. Delhi and Agra were the centres of power, while the present territories of Pakistan were on the periphery of their kingdoms. Some historians have tried to solve this problem by arguing that the history of Pakistan should start from 711-12 AD—the date of the Arab invasion of Sindh. Another approach suggests that the starting point should be 1947, the year of the birth of Pakistan. One example is Gul Shahzad Sarwar who, in his textbook, writes:

> Although Pakistan came into being on 14 August 1947, its roots go deep into the remote past. Its establishment was the culmination of the struggle by the Muslims of the South Asian subcontinent for a separate homeland of their own, and its foundation was laid when Muhammad bin Qasim subdued Sindh in 712 AD.[4]

There are problems regarding how to treat the Sikh rule in the Punjab. Furthermore, there is a vacuum in dealing with the colonial period. The only period that receives emphasis is the era of the Freedom Movement or the Struggle for Pakistan, and this period is also reflective of the official point of view, completely ignoring alternative interpretations.

We can well understand that such a lopsided and misinformed history cannot create a broad perspective in the minds of our young generation. Nor can such history be useful for finding a job in the market. In its present state the subject is dull, repetitive, and unattractive to students yearning for serious study. It is too court-oriented and is deficient in describing the fate of the people.

The Teaching of History

The quality of teaching of any subject depends on its teachers. In the case of Pakistan, the teachers who undertook the job of teaching in colleges and universities in the early stages after partition, were so involved in internal politics and intrigues that they did not have the time for academic responsibilities. In Sindh and Karachi universities, the departments of history were divided into General history and Muslim history just to accommodate two professors as heads of each department. The personal result was that neither a new or fresh curriculum was made, nor was a new system of examination evolved. No effort was made to train young teachers in research methodology or to encourage new ideas in the subject. Some of the teachers were able to receive foreign scholarships for higher education. Some of them returned to Pakistan while others preferred to remain abroad. Those who were unable to go abroad remained confined to the hackneyed routine of teaching, finding no opportunity to improve their qualifications.

During partition, Punjab University was the only institution of higher learning that Pakistan inherited. Sindh, Karachi, Peshawar, and Quaid-i-Azam universities were founded later. As a result of partition, the non-Muslim teachers migrated and left a vacuum that was filled by the scholars who came to Pakistan as immigrants. In the discipline of history, the historians who took the responsibility of teaching mostly specialised in medieval India or Muslim history. As they were trained in the colonial institutions, they retained the outdated and traditional outlook within history. They adopted the colonial syllabus that dealt with the political history of the successive ruling dynasties. MA students were asked to read Rushbrook William, Ishwari Prasad, Beni Prasad, and Jadunath Sarkar. Most of our universities and their affiliated colleges recommended the books which they themselves had studied as students. Interestingly, famous and internationally known historians from the Aligarh school of history are missing from the list such as Irfan Habib, Athar Ali, Harbans Mukhia,

Musaffar Alam, Iqtidar Alam Khan and Khaliq Ahmad Nizami, to name a few.

Many attempts have been made to revise the curriculum but as the teachers are not aware of the latest publications and research works, they recommend retaining the same syllabus with minor changes. The result is that a teacher focusses on the same topics repeatedly throughout his career without adding anything. Continuous repetition of a subject makes the teacher dull and leads to loss of interest. A significant result of this repetition is that in the annual examination, the examiner repeats the same questions. The students on the basis of this pattern evolve a formula; they take the previous five years' question papers and select 15 questions out of them to prepare for the examination. They are never disappointed, as they find in the examination papers the questions they have well prepared. For example, in medieval history, the following types of questions keep recurring: who was the real founder of a Muslim state in India: Qutbuddin Aibak or Iltutmish? Or, what was Balban's theory of kingship? What were the economic reforms of Alauddin? In the case of the Mughal period, the usual questions are: describe the condition of India before the invasion of Babur; explain the blunders of Humayun; explain Akbar's religious policies; write notes on Nurjahan and her role; describe Shahjahan's period as the golden period of the Mughals; and explain the war of succession between Aurangzeb and Dara Shikoh. As this period it taught with an ideological perspective, Ahmad Sirhindi and Shah Waliullah are added and regarded as important personalities from the point of view of examiners.

In the Muslim History group the syllabus is very simple: the life of the Holy Prophet (PBUH), the Pious Caliphs, the Umayyids and the Abbasid dynasties. The same courses are repeated from school through college and university. The same pattern is followed in other histories, whether

European, American, or the history of civilisation. It is an easy way for the teacher to do the job and for students to pass the examination. This method encourages teachers and students to use cheap textbooks and guides. For example, there was a time in the 1960s and 70s when a man named Mukarjee was popular among the history students of Pakistan. His books on the Indian, American, European, Greek and the Roman histories were a sure guarantee to pass the examination. Later, his place is taken over by a Mahajan whose books on all fields of history were very popular in Pakistan as well as in India. Their counterpart in Pakistan is K. Ali whose books on Indian and Muslim history are recommended by the teachers. The students of Muslim history use Dr. A. Hamid's book on Islamic history on all levels.[5]

At higher levels the students are not required to consult original sources. They depend heavily on secondary sources and cheap textbooks, and not on contemporary researches. Moreover, there is no tradition of inter-disciplinary discussions and consultations. Students at college level are not advised on how to write a research paper. There are no requirements for students to make presentations in the classroom for discussion and debate. In the absence of any discussion, students and teachers are not trained to respond to and challenge any criticism.

The reading list that is provided to students is inadequate. There is no training in methodology or in the methods to be used in citation and in developing a bibliography. At times there is no indication of the publisher, year and place of publication, or even the full name of the author. The list is generally short and does not contain recent research works.

Moreover, the overwhelmingly ideological approach makes the subject dull and uninteresting. As Pakistan is declared to be an ideological state, it has become incumbent upon teachers to teach accordingly. History is used by the state to defend its ideological boundaries rather than to create awareness among students. All the events or individuals that do not fit into the prescribed ideological framework, are excluded from the textbooks. For example, Akbar, as a ruler is condemned while Ahmad Sirhindi is extolled as the champion of Islam.[6]

The change in the medium of instruction from English to Urdu and Sindhi has rapidly deteriorated the standard of education, apart from creating and strengthening a dual class-oriented society. As there are no standard textbooks either in Urdu or Sindhi, students have no alternative except to rely on the low quality guides or cheap textbooks to pass their examinations. There are hardly any good textbooks in Urdu and Sindhi on European, Russian, American or British History.

The result is obvious. Those who graduate and acquire higher degrees in history find no employment other than teaching. As teachers they reproduce the knowledge that they learned to swallow as students. There is no process of production or creation of new knowledge in the discipline of history in Pakistan. Moreover, there are few opportunities for history graduates to adopt other professions because of their inadequate academic training. Some of them take it as an optional subject in competitive examinations, others use their knowledge of history in the media. The fact is that there is no academic market for history degree holders.

History Teaching at the School Level

History teaching at the school level is even more pathetic. After the Parition of 1947, the old system of education continued in which history and geography were independent subjects. There were old history textbooks that contained chapters on ancient Indian History and a brief survey of world civilisations. They provided overall basic knowledge of history. The change came during the period of Ayub Khan when in the 1960s American experts prepared a new Education Report for implementation by the government.[7] In the new report both history and geography were excluded from the school syllabus and replaced by the introduction of a new subject called 'Social Studies' of which history became a part. History writing in Pakistan further suffered because of bitter and unfriendly relations with India. The anti-India material is not only inculcated in the history textbooks but also in other subjects such as Urdu and English literature.

Provincial Textbook Boards and the Curriculum Wing of the Ministry of Education have the monopoly to prepare and publish textbooks on all subjects. This greatly damages the quality of books. Unqualified writers, who are not well versed in history, write most of them. By ignoring recent research and development and new findings, they repeat the same old versions of history. As Engels points out, 'he who writes history textbooks writes history'. Keeping this in view, authoritarian and orthodox governments successively monitor the writing of textbooks to propagate their ideology, leaving no option to students to know any alternative version. Most history textbooks give political accounts of different periods and rarely mention social and cultural aspects. By emphasising the role of individuals history writers create more heroes than a small nation requires. There are different categories of heroes: firstly, there are politicians, freedom fighters, and rulers; in the second category there are Sufi saints, *ulema*, and litterateurs; thirdly, after the 1965 war with India there are army men who gallantly fought for their country. All history textbooks are now heavily loaded with anti-Indian writings. The logical outcome, as a result of reading these textbooks, is that generation after generation is polluted with hatred, prejudice, and intolerance.

Research

Apart from teaching, research is an important aspect of any discipline. Research works produced suffer from many deficiencies. Firstly, students and teachers who engage in research work to get M.Phil. or Ph.D. degrees, are motivated towards getting higher teaching jobs and promotions. Teachers try to get their research papers published in journals, as it is a requisite condition for promotion to higher grades. Though the condition is to get them published in journals of international repute, this is not strictly observed and publications are accepted even if they are published in magazines and newspapers. In some cases, even letters of acceptance from dubious journals are accepted to consider a case for promotion of candidates. These research papers do not contribute much to the sum total of knowledge on this subject. As most of these research papers are below accepted standards, the candidates try to get them published in their own university journals.

If we analyse the topics, which are selected for M.Phil. and Ph.D. research, they are mostly on the Pakistan Movement. The pet themes are the contribution of an area, individuals or groups of people like students, women, *ulema*, etc., to the Pakistan Movement. The choice of topics in some cases might have also been influenced by patriotism. Furthermore, these topics served to strengthen the official version of history for the justification of partition, and the ideology of two nations. The researchers are unable to consult original sources on medieval Indian history or Islamic history owing to lack of knowledge of Persian and Arabic.

Very few theses have been written on medieval history, as it requires knowledge of Persian. The same applies to Islamic history where knowledge of Arabic is needed to consult the original sources. As there is no provision to teach these languages to students of history, they are not well equipped to do any research in these fields. Concerning history itself, no research has been done on this subject.

There are two trends in Pakistani historiography: one is to prove that the existing territories of Pakistan have never been a part of the Indian subcontinent except for 500 years and, therefore, they have a separate identity of their own. This theory was popularised after the separation of East Pakistan and an attempt was made to connect Pakistan with Afghanistan and Central Asia culturally, rather than with India. In the second trend, regional historians are trying to construct a history that could strengthen regional identity. This kind of historiography is essentially a response to a strong centre, and reflects the centralisation of historiography itself. Among the four provinces, this trend is very strong in Sindh, which claims that it has its own separate history. Based on this claim, it asserts its provincial autonomy. In regional histories, regional nationalism plays an important role in historical narratives.[8]

During the period of Ayub Khan an attempt was made to write a comprehensive history of Pakistan. The general editor of the project was I.H. Qureshi and the contributors were prominent historians of Pakistan. It is a good general narrative but failed to provide any new point of view, interpretation or insight into our history.

There is a new trend in historiography outside the universities. Prominent political families are hiring historians for writing the history of their families or of their ancestors in order to give them a dignified place in history. Such biographies, financed by interested groups, fail to evaluate the role or character of a family or individual correctly and objectively. There is another trend among retired bureaucrats and generals, who write autobiographies to justify their own roles in recent history. In most cases such history is more glorification of individuals than objective and corrective narration of historical facts. As their claims are not challenged, their version of history passes as true. Some of them even take away all the documents and material under their control for writing autobiographies, and in this way deprive future historians from getting access to the materials and sources.

Besides this, there are other serious problems for researchers. No attempt is made to set up libraries containing original and secondary material of different periods and aspects of history. It is almost impossible for a scholar to travel from one city to another in search of material in public and private collections. There is no central catalogue to guide the researchers about the material that is lying in different libraries. Material of great importance, which is lying in government departments such as judicial and revenue records, needs to be properly sorted and preserved. Most of the records are kept in bundles and sacks waiting for experts to sift and catalogue them. There is no fellowship or financial assistance available to researchers to travel abroad for the collection of material.

Professional Societies

After partition, some historians who migrated from India formed the Pakistan Historical Society at Karachi whose Secretary was Moin-ul-Haq. It began to publish the *Journal of the Pakistan Historical Society* that earned respect in the academic community. It also set a tradition of holding History conferences in which historians from different countries participated. However, gradually the activities of the society slowed down. There are a number of reasons for this. First of all, the society has been monopolised by a group, which did not allow others to become its members. The same people were elected repeatedly and no system was evolved to involve more people in its academic activities. Moin-ul-Haq remained its Secretary till his death. After him, the society no longer remained functional. Its library and journal were taken over by the Hamdard Foundation. Presently, the journal is published by the Foundation, but its academic standard is not so high. However, it is commendable that the Foundation publishes it regularly.

Several attempts were made to form an association of historians but every time it failed to materialise because of lack of interest and initiative. Some conferences have been organised by different universities but this inititative could not become an annual programme. In the absence of any association or society, historians have no forum where they can assemble and present their researches. They also do not have any opportunity to contact foreign professional associations and participate in international conferences. This drawback further reduces their capacity to take an interest in research.

Research Institutes

There are some research institutes for historical research set up by the central and provincial governments. The Pakistan Institute of Historical and Cultural Research was set up in Islamabad with the aim of promoting research activities. Initially, its working was quite satisfactory. It published many books on different aspects of South Asian history. But later on it could not maintain the quality of its research. It has announced the publication of a comprehensive history of Pakistan several times but the project has remained in the doldrums. It irregularly publishes one research journal in English and another in Urdu. Both have a limited circulation.

The Punjab University has set up the Research Society of Pakistan with the purpose of publishing original Persian sources on medieval Indian history. In the early period, 1960s to 70s, it published a number of edited manuscripts of importance. It also undertook to publish monographs on the history of the Punjab. However, in 1998 in the absence of funding, the Society was dissolved. It continues to publish a journal intermittently, but its articles have no academic standard.[9]

In Sindh, just after partition, the provincial government established the Sindhi Adabi Board for the promotion of history and culture. The Board published the original sources on the history and culture of Sindh. Some of them were translated into Urdu and Sindhi. The Board also planned to publish a comprehensive history of Sindh in nine volumes but only three volumes have been published so far. The prospect of publishing the rest is doubtful for lack of qualified contributions.[10]

In the Punjab, the former Urdu Markaz and now the Urdu Science Board and Majlis-i-Tarraqi Adab in their early period (1950s and 60s), published Urdu translations of the Persian sources on medieval Indian history. These were excellent translations. However, now both institutes have abandoned the task due to lack of funding. At Karachi University there is an Institute for Central Asian History, which has published some excellent manuscripts.[11]

Conclusion

The present analysis shows defects and shortcomings in the teaching and writing of history at educational institutions. As most of the research and teaching institutes are state-owned, the researchers and teachers lack freedom to pursue their task freely without state intervention. Scholars belonging to state institutions cannot participate in any conference or seminar abroad without getting a 'No Objection Certificate' (NOC) from the government agencies. From time to time there are directives from the government, as well as from the institutions, not to publish any article without prior permission.

History is not a popular subject in the ruling circles. There is an anti-history trend in the elite classes, which discourages research and promotion of the subject. The reason is that they are afraid of documentation of their misdeeds in history. To counter the 'history from above' approach, which excludes common people from the process of history, there is no alternative approach to 'history from below' to highlight the role of ordinary people in shaping history. Further, people are also tired of reading and listening to out-dated interpretations, which justify all the acts of the ruling classes and project them as heroes, while ignoring the common man. They are interested in knowing more facts and different points of view to understand 'real' history. History needs freedom from a near-total ideological grip to discover and unfold an objective narrative.

There are universities in other countries where scholars are engaged in research work on South Asian history. These universities and their research institutes have their own agenda. They select the topics that are related to their interest, and construct history from their own point of view. In the absence of our own contribution, students and scholars have to study and rely on the work done by foreigners. In this way, we look at our history from their prism. It is said that the one 'who controls the past controls the future'. We have been liberated from political colonisation, but control over knowledge production, is worse than political domination.

Notes

1. At the time the draft of this paper was completed, the author did not have the quantitative data on the development of the discipline of history. This data is now placed in Annex I of the paper.
2. For Annals see Peter Burke, *The French Historical Revolution,* Stanford University Press, 1990. For an excellent anthology on writing history see Peter Burke (ed.), *New Perspective on Historical Writings,* Pennsylvania State University, 1986.
3. M. Ikram Rabbani, *An Introduction to Pakistan Studies,* The Caravan Book House, Lahore, 1987, p. 10.

4. Gul Shahzad Sarwar, *Pakistan Studies,* Tahir Sons, Karachi, 1989, p. 44.
5. A. Hamid, *Tarikh-i-Islam* (Urdu), Lahore, n.d.
6. Mubarak Ali, 'Akbar in Pakistani Textbooks', in *History on Trial,* Fiction House, 1999, Lahore, pp. 76-82.
7. Report of the Commission on Education, 1959.
8. For a full discussion see Mubarak Ali, 'Pakistan's Search for Identity,' in Paul Brass and Achin Vanaik (eds.), *Competing Nationalisms in South Asia,* Orient Longman, Delhi, 2002; for the Sindhi point of view of history see G.M. Syed, *Sindh Jo Surma* (Heroes of Sindh), Hyderabad, Sindh (n.d.) and Abdul Waheed Arisar, *Ji Aim Saiyyad* (Sindhi), Munzurabad, n.d.
9. Some of the publications of the Research Society of Punjab University are: *Fatawa-i-Jahandari* by Ziauddin Barani; *Tarikh-i-Iradat Khan* by Iradat Khan; *Ruqqat-i-Abul Fath Gilani* by Abul Fath Gilani and *Diwan Dara Shikoh.*
10. Some of the publications of the Sindhi Adabi Board are: *Tarikh-i-Masumi, Tuhfatul Kiram, Maklinama, Tarikh-i-Mazhar Shahjahani.* The Board published the Urdu and Sindhi translations of *Cuchnama, Tarikh-i-Masumi and Tuhfatul Kuram.*
11. Some of the Urdu translations of the Urdu Markazi Board are: *Tarikh-i-Firuzshahi* by Ziauddin Barani; *Ma'thirul Umara* by Shahnawaz Khan and *Tabaqat-i-Akbari* by Bakshi Nizamuddin. Majlis-i-Tarraqi Adab's publications are: *Tuzuk-i-Jahangiri and Amal-Saleh* by Saleh Kambuh. Some of the publications of the Institute of Central and West Asian Studies are: *A Calendar of Documents on Indo-Persian Relations* (Vols. 1 and 2); *Central Asia: History, Politics and Culture* by Riazul Islam and *Khan-i-Khanan Nama* by Debi Prasad.

Annex I

The Quantitative Data on Development of the Discipline of History in Pakistan

The Number of Teachers and Their Qualifications

Opened in 1932, the Department of History of Punjab University is one of three departments of social sciences that Pakistan inherited from undivided India in 1947. A number of well-known historians, British, Indian and later Pakistanis, participated in its formation and later development.[1] By 1963, the number of history departments in public universities in Pakistan rose to six. They were located at Punjab University, Peshawar University, Karachi University and Sindh University, the latter two having two departments. By 2001, as recorded in the 2001 Handbook,[2] the number of history departments rose from 6 to 12. The six new departments were opened in Bahauddin Zakariya University, Balochistan University, Quaid-i-Azam University, Islamia University and Allama Iqbal Open University, the latter had two departments.

In the six departments reported by 1963, mentioned above, there were 36 teachers with an average of six teachers per department. By 2001, the number of teachers rose to 75 but the average per department remained about the same.

By 1963, the University of Karachi had the highest number of history teachers (7 General History and 7 Islamic History), followed by the University of Sindh (5 General History and 4 Muslim History). By 2001, while the University of Karachi retained its first position with 18 teachers, Sindh University lost its second position to Quaid-i-Azam University with 13 teachers. From among the total number of teachers of social sciences in 2001, 8 per cent teachers were of history, which is lower than three disciplines[3] and higher than 10 disciplines.[4]

According to the 1963 Handbook, out of the total 36 teachers of history at that time, 16 (44%) had Ph.D. degrees no teacher had an M.Phil. degree and 19 (53%) teachers were MAs.[5] By 2001, out of 75 total teachers 22 (29%) held Ph.D. degrees, 9 (12%) with M.Phil. degrees and the remaining 44 (50%) had MA degrees. The difference in share percentage of three degrees in 1963 and 2001 shows a decrease of 15% for Ph.Ds and an increase of 12% and 6% for M.Phil. and MA degrees respectively. These figures deviate from the general pattern of rise in Ph.D. teachers in most other social science disciplines.

Out of 36 teachers of history in 1963, 17 (47%) had their degrees from foreign universities. In 2001, out of 75 teachers 13 (17%) had such degrees showing 30% decline in foreign qualified teachers in 38 years. Considering Ph.D. separately, from among the 16 Ph.D. teachers 13 (81%) had foreign degrees. In 2001, out of the total 22 Ph.D. teachers 4 (18%) had their degrees from foreign universities, thus showing a 63% decline in the foreign trained Ph.Ds. The overall conclusion emerging from the above data is that the share percentage of Ph.D. teachers (total as well as foreign trained) and the total foreign qualified teachers has declined by the year 2001 as compared to 1963.

Ph.D. and M.Phil. Theses

For earning a professional degree at the level of Ph.D. and M.Phil. the completion of a thesis is a necessary requirement for a student. The quality and quantity of theses produced by a department reflect its academic strength as well as its contribution to the preparation of well qualified researchers who will be teaching or doing research in the discipline.

Since the emergence of the country up to 2001 (54 years) History departments in six public universities[6] have produced a total of 126 Ph.D. and M.Phil. theses. Out of them 43 (34%) are Ph.D. and 83 (66%) are M.Phil. theses. In these

54 years the average for Ph.D. theses is less than one per year and for M.Phil. theses is over two theses per year. Fifty eight (46%) theses were produced before 1987 and 68 (54%) were completed between 1987 to 2001.

Out of 43 Ph.Ds 25 were produced before 1987 (0.6 per year) and 18 from 1987 to 2001 (1.2 per year). Out of 83 M.Phil. theses 33 (40%) were completed before 1987 with an average of 0.9 per year and 50 (60%) from 1987 to 2001 with an average of three theses per year. This data suggests that production of both Ph.D. and M.Phil. theses in the first 39 years (counting from 1948 to 1986) was slower than during 15 years from 1987 to 2001.

Out of the total 43 Ph.Ds produced by seven universities by 2001, the University of the Punjab has produced the largest number (12), followed by Karachi University (9) and Quaid-i-Azam University (6). The remaining four universities[7] together have produced 16 Ph.D. theses. Out of the total 83 M.Phil. theses produced during the same period, Quaid-i-Azam University has produced the largest number (71), followed by Bahauddin Zakariya University (5). Punjab University and Islamia University have not produced any M.Phil. thesis. The remaining three universities[8] together have produced seven M.Phil. theses.

The decade-wise breakdown of Ph.D. theses shows that one thesis was produced in the 1940s, three theses were produced in the 50s, five in the 60s, ten in the 70s, 11 in the 80s and eight in the 90s. The decade-wise breakdown of M.Phil. theses shows that one M.Phil. thesis was produced in the 60s, 15 theses in the 70s, 31 in the 80s and 28 in the 90s. Eight M.Phil. theses were completed in 2001. It may be noted that there is a consistent increase in the number of M.Phil. theses from the 70s onwards. One possible explanation of this increase is the establishment of the History department in 1973 at Quaid-i-Azam University, which has contributed 71 (86%) M.Phil. theses out of a total of 83 theses.

Out of 126 theses produced by 2001, 118 were written in English, 5 in Urdu,[9] one in Sindhi and two in Arabic. Ninety-nine (79%) of the theses writers were males and the remaining 27 (21%) were females.

The number of Ph.D. theses produced by all the three inherited disciplines by 2001 (the other two are Economics and Political Science) shows that History has produced the lowest number of Ph.D. theses (43), while Political Science and Economics have produced 64 and 45 theses respectively. The figure for M.Phil. theses produced by the three inherited departments shows that by 2001 the departments of Economics produced 184, History 83 and Political Science 18, placing History at second position.

By grouping all the 126 theses into different categories, we find that 25 (20%) theses fall in the category of 'Politics of Pakistan' including political parties, constitution making, elections and Islamisation', 20 (16%) in the category of 'Regional History with most of them related to Sindh', and 17 (14%) theses fall in the category of 'Pakistan Movement and Rise of Muslim Consciousness in India'. Fifteen (12%) theses were written on 'Biographies of Prominent Personalities', 13 (10%) theses on 'International Relations' and 6 (5%) on 'Muslim Rulers in India'. Three (2%) theses were written on each of the following topics: 'Education and Educational Institutions', 'Kashmir' and 'Separation of East Pakistan'.

Notes

1. Notable among them are: J.F. Bruce, its first Professor, Dr. A.L. Srivastava, Prof. J.D. Ward, Dr. Ishtiaq Hussain Qureshi, Prof. Dilawer Hussain, Prof. Sheikh Abdur Rashid, Prof. Dr. Abdul Hamid, Dr. Zafarul Islam, and Dr. Zawar Hussain Zaidi.
2. For details about the UGC Handbooks, see footnote 10 in the introductory chapter of this book.

3. Economics (22%), Public Administration/Administrative Science (14%), Education (14%).
4. International Relations (7%), Political Science (6%), Psychology (6%), Sociology (6%), Pakistan Study (5%), Area Study (3%), Philosophy (3%), Social Work (3%), Defence and Strategic Studies (2%) and Anthropology (1%).
5. There was one teacher at that time whose qualification was local BA.
6. We have received the information about theses from the following six public universities; Quaid-i-Azam University, University of the Punjab, Karachi University, Bahauddin Zakariya University, Sindh University and University of Peshawar.
7. Sindh University (5), Bahauddin Zakariya University (5), Islamia University (5) and Peshawar University (1).
8. Sindh University (3), Peshawar University (2) and Karachi University (2).
9. Two were written in Islamia University and one each in Karachi University, Punjab University and Sindh University.

6

The *Khilafat* Movement: Islamisation of Politics

There is an assumption that the Muslims can only be mobilised politically if religion, and religious symbols are used. If it is true, it means that politics requires religion to survive and to play an active role in Muslim society. In the words of poet Iqbal if religion is separated from politics, it becomes tyranny. However, there are two aspects of the use of religion. In the case of despotic and authoritarian systems, where power is concentrated in the hands of an individual, such as a monarchy or dictatorship, the religious scholars (*ulema*) are used by them to support their political ends. There are many examples in history which show how the kings and rulers asked the *ulema* to issue *fatwas* (religious injunctions) in their favour or in support of their policies. The recent example in this regard is of Anwar Saadat of Egypt who got the religious sanction from the scholars of al-Azhar (a religious university of Egypt) to visit Israel, which they declared was in the interest of Islam. In such cases, the *ulema* play the role of subordinates to the rulers and dictators and religion is used for their political motives. In the other case, where there are some democratic traditions or institutions, the *ulema* take advantage to organise themselves on the model of political parties and assert their religious views in an attempt to subordinate politics. In this regard they face tremendous problems in dealing with the new ideologies and political concepts such as nationalism, socialism, secularism and democracy. In order to resolve these issues in the light of Islam, some *ulema* totally rejected these modern political ideas and systems as un-Islamic, while others Islamised them, with some modifications, in order to accommodate them in the Islamic structure.

The *Khilafat* movement could be analysed and judged under the circumstances when the colonial government allowed political parties to play their role within the framework that was granted by the government. The *ulema*, who were confined to their religious seminaries, got an opportunity to emerge from their isolation and take part in politics. That was the first time when they became active in the mass movement; they plunged into it with full religious fervour and vigour.

It may be mentioned here that Abul Kalam Azad was the first to strive to organise the *ulema* to participate in active politics. Believing that the Muslim community of India could be guided only by religious zeal, he founded *Hizbullah* (party of God) in 1913 for the *ulema* to participate in political matters and take the leadership into their hands.

An attempt is made in this paper to analyse the role of the symbol of *khilafat* in the Muslim community of India and how the *ulema* became an integral part of the political activities that subsequently subordinated politics to religion.

I

During the Sultanate period in India (1206–1526), some of the sultans sought the recognition of the Abbasid caliph to legitimise their rule; otherwise, the recitation of the name of the caliph in the *khutba* (sermon which is delivered on the occasion of Friday and Eid prayers) was just symbolic. The Mughal emperors did not recognise the Ottoman caliphs and asserted their own sovereignty in India. In the 18th century, when the East India Company established its political authority and the Mughal emperor had lost his political power, Tipu Sultan (1782-1799), sent an embassy to the Ottoman caliph requesting him to recognise him as a legitimate ruler of Mysore. By getting this recognition he wanted acceptance from his Muslim subjects and also from his rival Muslim rulers like the Nizam of Deccan who regarded him as an upstart. He got the recognition, but at the same time the British government also persuaded the caliph to issue a *fatwa* telling Tipu Sultaņ not to fight against the British.[1] The caliph gave recognition to Tipu Sultan as a legitimate ruler and simultaneously pursued him on the behest of the British to remain loyal to the East India Company. This shows the weakness and political imbecility of the Ottoman caliph.

Another example that shows that the Ottoman caliph was not regarded as a symbol of unity and as a protector of the Indian Muslims was, when Sayyid Ahmad (d.1831), leader of the *Jihad* movement, launched his holy war against the Sikhs and made an attempt to establish an Islamic state in the NWFP. He proclaimed himself as the caliph and *amir al-muminin* (leader of the Muslims) in 1826, ignoring the Ottoman caliph and his claim over the whole Muslim *ummah*. His own caliphate was short lived and was not even recognised by the majority of the Indian Muslims.

Interestingly, the British promoted the image of the Ottoman caliph in India for their own political motives. In 1857, during the Great Rebellion, they got a *fatwa* from the caliph exhorting the Muslims not to fight against the British. Sulvia G. Haim in the article entitled 'The Abolition of the Caliphate and its Aftermath', which is a part of Thomas Arnold's book on the caliphate, writes:

> The decline of Muslim rule in India especially after British occupation and the final victory of England over the Muslim Raj in the middle of the 19th century placed the Indian Muslims in a position of inferiority which made them search for a symbol of

strength and power. This, together with the growth of communication, brought them into greater contact with the Ottoman Caliph who was then conducting a clever form of propaganda which Britain came to encourage. Because of their enmity to Russia at the time, Britain adopted a pro-Ottoman line and promoted among the Indian Muslims loyalty to the Ottoman Caliph who, in his turn took advantage of the position by spreading his propaganda and exploiting the false notion of the Caliphate put out by the Europeans.[2]

II

This is how Indian Muslims slowly began to regard the Ottoman caliph as the head of the Muslim world. In the wake of Jamaluddin Afghani's Pan-Islamic movement, the Ottoman Caliph Sultan Abdul Hamid I (1876–1909) tried to use it to establish his political position in the Muslim world. Sir Sayyid, realising the danger of this extra territorial loyalty warned the Indian Muslims not to look to the caliph as their protector or defender and remain loyal to the British government in India. He had the experience of 1857 when the Muslim community suffered heavily and was looked upon by the British with suspicions. Therefore, his concern was to inculcate the loyalty for the British government among the Muslims to restore their credibility. He argued that where the caliph had no political authority he should not be recognised there as the defender and protector. As the Indian Muslims did not live under the Ottomans, they were not obliged to be loyal to the caliph and regard him as their sovereign.[3]

The catastrophe of 1857 was so great for the Indian Muslims that it took them a decade to recuperate. In 1867, for the first time, the *ulema* responded to counter the problems faced under the colonial rule. The foundation of the Deoband provided guidance to the Indian Muslims in religious matters. Its *dar-ul-Ifta* (Department for issuance of *fatwa*) issued religious instructions on all political, social, cultural, and economic matters. The *madrassa* became famous for traditional religious education and attracting students not only from all parts of India but also from the Muslim neighbouring countries. It gave the *ulema* an opportunity to create a position for themselves as religious guides and instructors to the community. They resisted modernity and conserved the traditions which they regarded essential for the religious identity of their community.

On the other hand, Sir Sayyid, believing in modernity and progressive ideas, founded Aligarh College to educate the Muslims on modern lines and prepare them to cooperate with the British government. Both Deoband and Aligarh remained aloof from politics in their first phase. Their major concern was to rehabilitate the Muslims in the aftermath of 1857. However, a change of political situation also brought a change in the outlook of the Muslims. In 1906 when the Muslim League was founded, a sizeable European educated Muslim middle class had emerged with the ambition to acquire social status and political rights in the colonial structure. They controlled the new party in order to use it for their political gains. In the first phase, the Muslim League expressed loyalty to the British government and averted any resistance or opposition. However, the annulment of the partition of Bengal at home and the war between Turkey and Italy in 1911 changed their political strategy from loyalty to resistance against the British government. This change is pointed out by Mr. Patrie, the Assistant Director of the Intelligence Bureau, who in his Report (1912) writes:

> ... the belief held up to that time by Muslims in India, that the British government was a safe custodian of Islamic interests, was rapidly evaporating; and further that a rumour was gaining credence to the effect that the Christian powers had set themselves of deliberate purpose to encompass the ruin of Islam, with which object Great Britain had entered into a secret alliance with Italy

with respect to the latter's attack on Turkey. He pointed out that the belief in this rumour had been strengthened by the re-union of Bengal at the end of 1911, which was viewed with dismay by Bengali Muslims.[4]

During this period of political chaos and crisis, the Indian Muslims sympathised with Turkey. Azad's *al-Hilal, al-Bilagh,* Muhammad Ali's *Hamdard* and *Comrade,* and Zafar Ali Khan's *Zamindar* played an important role to promote these feelings. In 1912, a medical mission under Dr. Ansari went to Turkey to help the Turkish army. In 1913, an organisation *Anjuman Khuddam-i-Kaaba* was organised for the protection of the Muslim holy places against the danger of European attack. On the eve of the First World War, the Indian Muslims did not want Turkey to join the war against the Allies. However, the Ottoman government declared *jihad* (holy war) against the Allied powers and issued a *fatwa* to fight against the Allied powers. The real shock actually came when Turkey was defeated, and it appeared, that the Allied powers were going to dismember it. This made the Ottoman empire as a religious symbol to the Indian Muslims.

The reason was that the European powers had conquered and occupied nearly the whole Muslim world except for Turkey that retained its independence in spite of its weakness and misadministration. The Indian Muslims never felt the need to identify with the glories of the Ottomans as long as the Mughals were in power. The loss of power and complete elimination of the Mughal dynasty turned them to look to the Ottoman empire and find solace in its pomp and glory. Even Sir Sayyid, who opposed any pan-Islamist views, remarked: 'Once there were many Muslim kingdoms and we did not feel much grief when one of them was destroyed; now that so few are left, we feel the loss of even a small one. If Turkey is conquered that will be a great grief, for she is the last of the great powers left to Islam'.[5] On the eve of the Balkan wars, the Muslims of India became more conscious about the survival of Turkey. They started to relate Islam with Turkey so that any danger to Turkey became a danger to Islam.

III

During the First World War, both the Congress and the Muslim League tried to cooperate with each other and sort out those problems that had created a gulf between the two communities. As a result the Lucknow Pact of 1916 was signed in which Jinnah played a very active role. So far Muslim politics was not religious but liberal and assertive. Its aim was to get political concessions for the Muslims. The *khilafat* was not a major issue to dominate the political scene. However, the end of the war, the defeat of Turkey, and the revolt of the Arabs against the Ottoman imperialism with the help of European powers, created uneasiness among the Muslim middle classes. The turning point was the Delhi session of the Muslim League (1918) where Dr. Ansari, who was the chairman of the reception committee, invited the *ulema* in order to get their support. The leading *ulema*, accepting the invitation, were delighted to come at par with the modern educated Muslim leadership. The following statement of Maulvi Kifayatullah shows this quite clearly:

> I have always been of the opinion that the religion and politics of Muslims were one and the same thing. In fact their religion was their politics and their politics was their religion. So far they had thought that the Muslims had committed their religion to the custody of the *ulema* and their politics to the custody of the All India Muslim League and kindred organisations; but when they went out to them (the *ulema*) they came out with open arms and pleasure to join the political body.[6]

Chaudhary Khaliquzzaman, a Muslim leader from Oudh, realising the danger of Islamisation of politics warned: 'They would either be swept off their feets or would carry the whole of Muslim India with them'.[7] This is exactly what happened. The *khilafat* issue became the core issue of Muslim politics and all other problems were completely forgotten. Once *khilafat* became the symbol and religion was involved in it, the modern and liberal leadership was marginalised and the *ulema* as the custodians of religion came forward to lead the Muslim community of India. Ali brothers, who started their political career as moderates, were converted in the process and became *maulana* with beards and wearing the clothes worn by the religious leaders.

The important aspect of this period is that the entire political process was taken over by the All India *Khilafat* Committee that was set up in 1919 and made the Muslim League a non-entity. With the entry of *ulema*, the whole character of the movement changed. The element of emotionalism was fully inculcated to mobilise the Muslim masses in the name of religion. Fiery speeches with charged sentiments became daily occurrences. The study of the newspapers of this period clearly show the emotionalism. For example, Maulana Abdul Bari from Faringi Mahal who used to warn his rivals, threatened to eliminate them. In one of the Muslim League sessions, at Delhi he said that he could shake the world with one word of his mouth and one stroke of his pen.[8] At the Amritsar session of the Muslim League which was attended by the Ali brothers, emotional speeches were delivered. Shaukat Ali declared that he would sacrifice his property and life to protect Kaaba. He finished by asking the audience whether they wished to remain British subjects or Muslims, and if it was the former, he would sever his connection with them and seek martyrdom.[9]

As far as the question of Gandhi's support to the *Khilafat* movement is concerned, Gail Minault points out that Muhammad Ali was much impressed by Gandhi's approach to politics. Addressing students at Calcutta he said that 'politics cannot be divorced from religion'.[10] Gandhi was approached by Maulana Bari to support the *Khilafat* movement. That was the time when Gandhi planned to launch a campaign against the Rowlatt Bill and against the Punjab atrocities. It appears that it was easy for Gandhi to deal with the Ali brothers and *ulema* rather than Jinnah who was not in favour of the *khilafat* issue. The Congress and the *Khilafat* movement supported non-cooperation, and as a result a unanimous *fatwa* was issued by the *ulema* in 1920 that called upon the Muslims to boycott the government on religious grounds. The opening paragraph said:

> '*Mavalat*' is forbidden (*haram*) with enemies of Islam in both senses of the word. God has forbidden '*mavalat*' totally with enemies of Islam whether it is openly or secretly, paid or honorary. God says (Arabic verse) 'God prevents you from friendship and cooperation with those infidels who fought with you in matters of religion and ejected you from your countries and helped in your ejectment and expulsion. Those who cooperate with such infidels are tyrants'.[11]

During the whole movement, Gandhi became the supreme leader and highly praised by the Ali brothers and the *ulema*. However, the non-cooperation movement collapsed after the *Chaura Chauri* incident in 1922 and the *khilafat* issue became redundant when Mustafa Kamal abolished the institution in 1924.

IV

The *Khilafat* movement Islamised the politics of the Indian Muslims. Instead of creating political understanding and analysing political issues purely on political grounds, they supported or rejected all these issues on the basis of religion. Once religion became the supreme authority to understand and act politically, the *ulema* gained ground and assumed leadership. This is evident during the *Khilafat* movement when attempts were made to establish a separate *shariat* court and collect *zakat*. The movement as a result created religious and non-political consciousness among the Muslims. The Congress, on the other hand, followed the political agenda that promoted the political awakening among its followers (the majority of them were Hindus).

The Muslim community under the spell of religious leadership also failed to understand the impact of Ottoman imperialism on the Arab countries. The news of the Arab revolt when received in India was not believed. This lack of political knowledge failed to create anti-imperialist feelings among the Muslims. It is evident that even educated Muslims were not well aware of the Ottoman history and its decadent institutions, which were not based on Islamic teachings. It was just an emotional attachment that blinded them to probe and investigate the weaknesses of the Ottoman empire.

According to one interpretation involvement in the *Khilafat* movement was nothing but a waste of the Indian Muslims' energies. They forgot their internal problems and devoted their attention to the problem which was not related to them. That is why there was disappointment after the abolition of the *khilafat*. It left the Muslims in the wilderness.

According to another interpretation the *Khilafat* movement was not only for the protection of the institution of the caliphate but by being anti-British, it was aimed to activate the Muslims to participate in Indian politics. Mushirul Haq, defending Azad, argues that 'Azad had a definite political programme in mind; he wanted to drag the *ulema* into the political struggle; he also wanted to incite Muslims to action against the British in the name of religion'.[12] Gail Minault in her study on the *Khilafat* concludes that the movement made all sections of the society active. Labourers, women, students, and common people were all involved in all sorts of political activities, agitation, demonstrations and boycott. The *Khilafat* and the non-cooperation both brought Hindus and Muslims together.[13]

The Hindu-Muslim unity was short lived because it was based on emotionalism and not on political pragmatism. After the collapse of non-cooperation, Gandhi was criticised and condemned by the same *ulema* who adored him. It is said that he used the Muslim leadership to propagate his non-violence philosophy and left them in the doldrums when he achieved his motives. Both the symbols *Khilafat* and non-cooperation were quite different in nature and could not be reconciled. The nationalist historians, who admire Gandhi's role as a champion of Hindu-Muslim unity during this period, forget the disastrous effects of the involvement of religion into politics. Two incidents show it: Maulana Abdul Bari and Azad both issued a *fatwa* declaring Hindustan as a *darul harb* (home of war) and therefore exhorted the Muslims that it was their religious duty to migrate from India. The common people especially from the Punjab and Sindh, after selling their belongings, left India for Afghanistan where the *Amir* also promised to give them land and shelter. Once they reached there they found nothing and came back disappointed. During the whole campaign hundreds died and thousands suffered in the process of rehabilitation. Those who issued the *fatwa* did not follow it; both the rich and well off did not leave India. The sacrifice of the common people did not create any concern among the leadership. In the second incident, the Mopla peasantry revolted against their landlords. Economic exploitation forced them to rebel repeatedly in the past. Now inspired by the symbol of the *khilafat,* they took arms and made attempts to improve their condition. The revolt was crushed and the Moplas suffered immensely. In this case nothing was done to ameliorate their grievances.

One of the features of the *Khilafat* movement was its appeal for donations for a religious cause. The major donors were the Muslim seths of Bombay who actively took part in the movement. The masses gave donations whenever they were appealed to at public meetings. The leadership toured throughout the country to mobilise people for the cause and asked them to donate liberally. Musarrat Husain Zuberi writes about such a visit in his hometown Marehra: 'The vivid recollection is still there of the wonderful oratory of Maulana Hamid and his brother Majid Badauni that night. The electrified atmosphere was good for the Khilafat chest. The ladies from behind the curtain took off whatever jewellery they had on and we the young boys collected them and presented them to the *Maulvis*'.[14] However, at the end when the account was audited it was found that there was misuse of funds and also embezzlement. It discredited the leadership, and led to a sad end of the movement.

The *Khilafat* movement, as a matter of fact, was the result of the emerging Muslim middle class who, in search of their identity, relied on Islam. The *khilafat* issue provided them an opportunity to assert their separate identity. The common Muslims had no interest in this issue and were involved marginally. However, the result of the whole process was that religion became an integral part of the Muslim politics in India. Even when the *ulema* were eclipsed after the collapse of the movement, the modern and liberal the Muslim leadership was forced to use religion to mobilise the masses for political purposes.

One question remains whether the British government in India secretly supported the *Khilafat* movement. One explanation could be that after the Treaty of Sevres 1920, the weak caliph suited the British and the Allied powers more than Mustafa Kamal who was adamant not to accept the peace terms. The delegation of Justice Amir Ali and the Aga Khan to go to Turkey to advocate the cause of the caliphate created some doubts. In the words of W.C. Smith: 'The Turkish Ghazi was irritated to see men like Amir Ali and His Highness Aga Khan approaching him on the subject of the Turkish and the Islamic constitutions: he pointed out with some scorn their inimate and friendly relations with British imperialism'.[15] However, not having any evidence it is difficult to prove anything.

Once the institution of *khilafat* was abolished, different Muslim rulers made attempts to revive it, but they could not so despite many efforts. However, the romantic image of the *khilafat* survives even today. It is believed that it was the best system to solve all political and economic problems of Muslim society. We can also see the continuity of the impact of the *Khilafat* movement on the present politics of the Indian subcontinent where fundamentalism is gaining ground and liberal forces are receding to the background.

Notes

1. I.H. Qureshi, 'Tipu Sultan's Embassy to Constantinople, 1787', in *Haider Ali and Tipu Sultan*, Irfan Habib (ed.), Tulika, Delhi, 1999, pp. 69-78.
2. S.G. Haim, 'The Abolition of the Caliphate and its Aftermath', in *The Caliphate* by T.W. Arnold, OUP, Karachi, 1966, pp. 137-8.
3. Sir Saiyyid, *Maqalat*, Vol. I, Majlis Tarraqi Adab, Lahore, 1966, p. 157.
4. P.C. Bamford, *Histories of Khilafat and Non-cooperation Movements*, K.K. Books, Delhi (reprinted), 1985, p. 110.
5. B.R. Nanda, *Gandhi: Pan-Islamism, Imperialism, and Nationalism in India*, OUP, Delhi, 1989, p. 108.
6. *Ibid.*, p. 207.
7. *Ibid.*
8. P.C. Bamford, *op. cit.*, pp. 133-4.
9. *Ibid.*, p. 140.
10. G. Minault, *The Khilafat Movement: Religious Symbolism and Political Mobilisation in India*, OUP, Delhi, 1982, p. 56.
11. P.C. Bamford, *op. cit.*, p. 252.
12. M.U. Haq, *Muslim Politics in Modern India*, Book Traders, Lahore (n.d.), p. 100.
13. G. Minault, *op. cit.*, pp. 210-11.
14. M.H. Zuberi, *Voyage through History*, Vol. I, Hamdard Foundation, Karachi, 1987, p. 60.
15. W.C. Smith, *Modern Islam in India*, Lahore (reprinted), 1947, p. 348.

7

Religion and Politics: Integration, Separation and Conflict

Both religion and politics have one common goal: that is to acquire political power and use it to fulfil their aims. However, to achieve this object, their methods are different. Religion mobilises the religious sensibilities of people in order to get their support to capture power; while politics uses intrigue, diplomacy, and makes an attempt to win public opinion either democratically, if the system allows it, or usurps power with the help of the army, if the society is under-developed and backward. Therefore, in the power struggle, both politics and religion make attempts to undermine each other. If religion holds political authority, its ambition is to exploit it to fulfil a divine mission. It claims that it derives authority from divinity and therefore its mission is holy, motivated to reform society under spiritual guidance. Politics, on the contrary, bereft of any value, directs its policy to the needs and requirements of society whereupon, it is obliged to change laws and the system of government accordingly. This is a basic difference between two approaches of religion and politics: religion determines its authority on divine laws which could not be changed with human intervention; while in a pragmatic political approach society should move ahead, change and adapt itself to the new arising challenges of time. In its secular approach man is responsible to determine his destiny. He is not under the control of divinity to remain submissive and inactive. On the contrary, he is supposed to initiate and plan to build a society according to his vision.

There are three models in history related to religion and politics. In one when religion and politics both unite with each other in an attempt to monopolise political power. We call it integration and sharing model. In the second model, politics after subduing and overpowering religion, uses it for its interests. In this model religion plays a subservient role to politics. In the third model both come into conflict with each other that subsequently lead to their separation. In this model they appear as rivals and compete to struggle for domination.

The study of the beginning and spread of any religion shows that every religion is started in particular space and time; therefore, the main focus of its teachings is the solution of existing problems. However, with the change of time there are new challenges and a religion has to respond to them for its survival. In this process, it has to adjust its teachings according to changes. With the passage of time, a stage comes when a religion fails to respond to challenges of its time and finds hardly any space to adjust according to new environments. For example, in the case of Islam, it took nearly two and a half centuries to complete its orthodoxy. Once the process was complete, it became impossible for orthodoxy to give any place to new ideas and new thinking. It was believed that any change in the structure would weaken its base. On this plea it persists in retaining its old structure without any addition.

At this stage there remain three options for any religion.

1. Avoid and disapprove any change in its structure. If any attempt is made to reinterpret its teachings, such attempts are either crushed politically or with the help of religious injunctions (*fatwa* in the case of Islam). Those who claim to reconstruct religious thoughts should be condemned as enemies of religion and

believers should be warned to boycott them and not listen to their views.

2. In the second option, religion has a choice to adapt itself according to the needs of time and accept new interpretations relating to its teachings and accommodating modernity.
3. In the third option, if religion fails to respond to the challenges and feels insecure, it withdraws from active life and decides not get entangled in worldly affairs. It confines its activities to spirituality.

The helplessness of religion is obvious in the present circumstances in which scientific and technological inventions are rapidly changing the society and its character making it more complex and mechanical. Especially, with the extension of knowledge, politics, economics, sciences, technology and other branches of knowledge assume a separate entity that could be specialised and handled by professionals. *Ulema* or religious scholars are not in a position to understand the intricacies of these professions and adjust them with religious teachings. This is the reason why in some societies religion is separated from politics and economics and it no more enjoys the domination over the society, which it did in the medieval period.

The characteristic of three reactions may be defined as aggressive, compromising, and separatist respectively.

There are groups of people in every society who want change in their practical life but at the same time they desire not to abandon religion. These people become supporters of new interpretations of religion that suits their way of life. It causes emergence of new sects. Therefore, we find that in every religion, there are new sects, which fulfil the demands of a group of people within a span of time and then disappear in the oblivion of history. However, some sects persist and survive. For example, in Christianity, when the bourgeoisie wanted religious sanction of interest, Calvin (d.1594), a religious reformer, allowed it on the basis of religion. It removed business hurdles and the merchant and industrial classes flourished. R.H. Tawney, in his classical book *Religion and the Rise of Capitalism* rightly says, 'Calvin did for the bourgeoisie of the 16th century what Marx did for the proletariat of the 19th...'.

I

In Islamic history, conflict between religion and politics settled after the Abbasid revolution (750 AD) when the Iranians, who made the revolution a success and subsequently assumed a position of power and authority in the government administration, formulated the state policy of their liking. They wanted to make the Abbasid Caliph just like the Persian monarch having absolute political power with religious authority: a combination of temporal and spiritual powers. The Iranian bureaucracy was opposed by the *ulema* who strove to curtail the power of the caliph in view of the *shariat* (religious laws). As the Iranians had political and military support, they cornered the *ulema* in their efforts and made the caliph a Persian king along with all royal symbols and rituals which once prevailed at the Sassanid court. However, it was settled that in practice the caliph would remain absolute in administrative and political matters but he would not interfere in the affairs of the *shariat* nor would he make any effort to change it. It would remain the domain of the *ulema*. It is how religion and politics separated from each other in the early stage of Islamic history.[1]

As a result of this settlement, a system emerged in which the ruler had unlimited power. Professional bureaucracy to administer the state and its affairs supported him. The *ulema* joined the state as *qazi* (judge), *mufti* (interpreter of law), *muhtasib* (ombudsman) and as *imam* (prayer leader). In these capacities they became servants of the state and as such their responsibility was to obey the ruler and state and interpret the *shariat* according to the interest of the caliph. Once the economic interests of the *ulema* were linked to the state as they received either stipends or *jagirs* (fiefs) from the state, their main concern was to please the ruler. On the other hand, rulers also adopted a policy of conciliation towards them. They showed outward respect to them; invited them to their court to deliver sermons and asked for their advice on important issues. However, whenever, they wanted to use these *ulema* for their political interest; they asked them to issue *fatwas* in their favour, which they obliged with pleasure. We find that is how these *ulema* religiously justified the Persian court ceremonies of prostration before the ruler, kissing his feet or hands and addressing him with high-sounding titles. They also helped rulers if they wanted to avoid religious duties such as obligatory daily prayers and fasting in the month of Ramazan.To get sexual pleasure, rulers got religious sanction by the *ulema* to marry and divorce as they liked and to keep as many slave girls as they wished. During the Abbasid period, as the power of the Caliph increased, influence of the *ulema* decreased and they ultimately became subservient to the ruler and his whims.

II

With the decline of the Abbasids, provincial ruling dynasties emerged and introduced the institution of the sultanate (kingship). Muslim jurists justified it on the plea that it would prevent chaos and keep law and order in the society. Secondly, they also legitimised the usurption of power by powerful military man arguing that to reject him meant to create political unrest and a situation of civil war. Al-Marwardi (d.1058) was the political thinker who in his book *al-Ahkam al-Sultania* advises that a usurper should be recognised as legal ruler just to avoid bloodshed.[2] After settling the issue of kingship and usurper, the question was whether a ruler should remain under religious authority or should he use religion for his political motives? To respond to this question and how the king should behave, a genre of literature was produced known as the 'Mirror of Princes'. Some of the important books are *Qabusnama* by Kaikaus (d.1082), *Siyasatnama* by Nizamulmulk Tusi (d.1091) *Nasihat al-Muluk* by Ghazali (d.1111), and *Fatawa-i-Jahandari* by Ziauddin Barani. In this literature, kingship was recognised as a hereditary institution and the ruler was addressed as '*Zill-I-Ilahi*' (shadow of God). It was a Machiavellian step that freed the king from all religious bindings and made him authoritative and powerful. Similarly, the '*Adab*' or the literature of the Mirror of Princes made the Muslim king free from the *shariat* and allowed him to rule absolutely. Their model was the Sassanid king who was all-powerful: in religion as well as worldly matters. However, an attempt was made to control the authority of the ruler by asking him to follow a policy of justice like Anushirwan, the legendary king of Persia, who was famous for his benevolence and acts of justice. The method was to control absolute power by asking him to follow and adhere to moral and ethical values in order to govern people.

In India, the Sultans of Delhi (1206-1526) adopted this model but the Mughal king Akbar shaped a different theory of kingship which suited the Indian environment. Abul Fazl (d.1602), the court historian and close friend and advisor to Akbar provided the philosophical basis for Mughal kingship by exalting the position and emphasising the importance of royalty. Royalty, according to him, was the highest dignity in the eyes of God. It was light which emanated from God. He calls it 'the Divine Light'. This light created paternal love for his subjects in the king's heart and increased his trust in God.[3]

Commenting on the Mughal concept of kingship, Vanina writes that apparently this theory does not seem different from the Islamic or Hindu theories of kingship. However, a deeper study reveals that it is not the same but quite different from the previous traditions. According to Abul Fazl, the king rules for the welfare of his subjects and to achieve this he has the right to change ancient traditions and communal institutions. As royalty emanates from God, the king does not need to follow the advice of the *ulema* or religious scholars. He is authorised by the divine power to bring changes in the social structure according to the need of the times. Akbar did it. He banned child marriages and marriages among close relatives. He also banned *sati*, though he could not eliminate it altogether. In this respect, Akbar was the first Indian ruler who interfered in the affairs of community, caste, and family that were otherwise taboo for rulers to talk about or change them.[4]

Akbar further extended his power when his *sadr al sadur* (highest religious post at the Mughal court) ordered the execution of a Brahman on the charges of blasphemy. On this occasion Akbar asked Abul Fazl's father Shaikh Mubarak to guide him on how to get rid of the *ulema*. The Shaikh suggested that Akbar should assume the authority of *mujtahid* with the approval of the *ulema*. Akbar following his advice asked the *ulema* to sign a *mahzar* (so-called decree of infallibility) delegating him authority to interpret religion. This combined in him religious as well as political powers and the *ulema* lost their authority to challenge the royal decision.

Ziauddin Barani, a historian of the Sultanate period, explains his theory of kingship in his book *Fatawa-i-Jahandari* that it is very difficult for a king to rule following the *shariat*. According to him there is a difference between the *shariat* and the rules and regulations of kingship. It is important for a king to keep and preserve his grandeur, pomp and glory. He should observe all court ceremonies such as prostration, and the kissing of hands and feet by courtiers. He should live in palaces, keep his treasury full with all types of wealth and use it for his own personal needs. All such acts are justified on the ground that a king without display of power and glamour is not respected by his subjects.[5]

In this regard, Ziauddin Barani quotes a dialogue between Alauddin Khilji (1296-1316) and Qazi Mughis in the *Tarikh-i-Firuzshahi.* When the king asked the *qazi* about his policies whether they were according to the *shariat* or not, the *qazi* replied in the negative. On it, the response of the king was that he did not know anything about the *shariat*. He did what he thought was good for his subjects.[6]

Therefore, Muslim rulers in order to rule did not follow the *shariat* but formulated their own rules and regulations that were in favour of practical politics. As he was the shadow of God *(Zilli-i-Ilahi)* and deputy to God, those who rebelled against him were regarded as his personal enemies and were punished likewise. They were not judged according to the *shariat* but on the basis of the king's anger. Sometimes, they were hacked to pieces, and sometimes were trampled under the feet of an elephant. Alauddin Khilji not only punished the rebels but also in retaliation their family members including women and children were imprisoned, tortured and enslaved. According to Barani the custom to imprison women and children of rebels as a punishment was started by him that was continued later on by other rulers.[7]

Under this model of kingship, *muftis* (jurists) and *qazis* (judges) became servants to the state and as such served the interest of rulers rather than implementation of the *shariat*. They issued *fatwas* whenever needed by the ruler to justify their acts. There are many such examples in history. One interesting *fatwa* was regarding legitimising Akbar's marriages. He married more than four wives and when it was pointed out that his extra marriages were illegal, he asked the *ulema* to find a solution. The matter was discussed in the *Ibadatkhana* (house of worship) which was founded by him in 1575. The result was that one religious scholar interpreted that in the holy Quran there is the verse which says to marry: 2, 3 and 4 which according to him was 2+3+4=9. Another scholar's interpretation was 2+2+3+3+4+4=18. However, Abdul Qadir Badauni, the historian, suggested that as in the Malki school of jurisprudence *muta* (temporary marriage) was legal and a *qazi* of the Malki school could legalise his marriage after issuing such a *fatwa*. Akbar was pleased with this suggestion. He immediately appointed a Malki *qazi* who forthwith issued the *fatwa* to legalise his extra marriages. Akbar, after getting the *fatwa* dismissed the *qazi* from the post. He did not want the others to take advantage of it.[8]

When Aurangzeb (1658-1707) executed Dara Shikoh and Murad, his two brothers, he made their execution religious and not political. Dara was condemned to death on the charges of atheism and Murad on the basis of *qisas* (revenge for homicide). Though everybody knew that he wanted to get rid of his brothers because they were claimants to the throne. He used religion to fulfil his political motives and the *ulema* readily issued a *fatwa* according to his wishes.

In another incident when he was in the Deccan besieging the fort of Satara, four Muslims and nine Hindus were brought as prisoners of war. He asked the *qazi* for a *fatwa*. He told the king that if the Hindus were to convert to Islam they should be released and the Muslims should be kept in prison, as punishment. Aurangzeb did not approve of this *fatwa* because he wanted to punish all of them and reprimanded the *qazi* that instead of the Hanafi school of jurisprudence, he should find other jurists for a different opinion. The *qazi* understood that the king wanted severe punishment and issued another *fatwa* recommending that both the Muslims and the Hindus should be executed.

On one side, Aurangzeb used religion for political purposes but when religious elements made attempts to use politics for their advantage he resisted it. For example when he was asked to expel the Hindus and the Shias from his administration, his reply was that religion and politics were two separate things and they should not be mixed with each other. Similarly, when a *qazi* refused to recite the *khutba* in his name on the plea that his father, emperor Shah Jahan, was alive, he dismissed him and appointed a *qazi* of his liking. Later on when some *ulema* opposed his invasion to the Deccan states as the Muslim kings ruled them, he did not bother about their opinion; neither did he bother when a religious scholar reprimanded him in public about why he did not marry his daughters.[9]

Against this model of kingship in which the ruler became absolute, there were different movements to bring political authority under the *shariat*. One and the significant movement in this regard was of Imam Hanbal (d.855) who opposed the 'mu'tazilah' and Mamun's campaign of the 'creation of the Quran'. He underwent severe torture but persisted in his opinion. His followers were very strict in matters of *shariat* and during the Abbasid period they rioted in different cities demanding the implementation of the rule of *shariat*. For example, they used to visit the bazaar of Baghdad and harass the shopkeepers for not observing religious rules. They destroyed wine shops and threatened people not to dance or sing. It was also common to attack opponents for their views. Those caliphs who ignored their warning also became their victims. They publicly exhorted people to revolt against them.[10]

The second important movement was of Ibn Taymmiya (d.1328). He belonged to the Hanbali school of jurisprudence and wanted the *ulema* to play an effective role in political affairs. The main thrust of his movement was that instead of rulers, the *ulema* should be given powers to implement the *shariat*. In India, the Mahdawi movement, which was started by Sayyid Mahdi Jaunpuri in the 15th century, wanted to purify Islam in India and establish an ideal Islamic society. In the 16th century, the movement became very popular in Gujarat but soon lost its popularity because of its extremism and was finally confined to its own *da'ira* or circle.

All such movements, which challenged the authority of Muslim rulers, were crushed with an iron hand as no ruler tolerated any challenge against his power. Though such movements challenged the divine concept of kingship and his absolute power but at the same time they failed to win the support of people because of their fanatical attitude and ultimately collapsed without changing the state structure.

III

In the second model of the state religion dominates politics and uses it for implementation of its practices. There were two types of religious domination over politics. In one case, a ruler, in the interest of his rule and stability of his ruling dynasty, implements the *shariat* and allows the *ulema* to play a leading role in the state affairs. In the second category, the *ulema*, after capturing political power, establish a religious state and force people to follow their religious agenda. Such religious states, wherever, they were founded in the West or in the East, basically believed that human beings could be reformed only by coercion and control over their actions. Therefore, to set up a purified society, strict and exemplary punishments were given for minor crimes. It was also believed that worldly rulers were corrupt and evil-minded. Therefore, only religious scholars could rule with honesty and work for the welfare of people.

One of its examples is the city-state of Geneva that was established by the Christian reformer Calvin (d.1599). After acquiring political power, he was in a position to realise his religious ideals. The first thing he did was an announcement that those who were not in favour of his religious ideas should leave the city. Those who stayed back faced his rigorous disciplinary action on different offences including excommunication from Christianity; exile from the city; imprisonment, and death penalty. On his order all hotels and guesthouses, which provided sexual facilities to the guests, were closed. Those traders and shopkeepers who were found involved in adulteration or weighing less were severely punished. Vulgar songs and playing cards were prohibited. Care was taken that the Bible should be available at all important places. Those who were found laughing during a sermon were reprimanded; it was obligatory for every citizen to thank God before eating. As a result of these strenuous laws, every individual and family in Geneva was completely under the control and supervision of Calvin's spiritual police. Punishments were severe and no concessions were made to exempt anybody. Once a child was beheaded for the crime that he struck his father. It is said that during the period of 6 years 150 heretics were burnt alive. The result was that the citizens of Geneva were soon fed up of this system and ended it after expelling Calvin from the city.[11]

In the Islamic world we could see this model in Najad and Hijaz where in the 18th century a religious movement erupted and soon engulfed the whole region. Its founder Muhammad Ibn Abdul Wahab (d.1792) launched the campaign to purify Islam from irreligious practices. Muhammad Ibn Saud, the founder of the Saudi ruling dynasty, was influenced by his teachings that made matrimonial alliances with his family. When one of the members of his dynasty, Saud (d.1814) defeated his rivals and established his rule he made the Wahabi religious ideas his state religion. As Wahabi believed in revivalism and purity of religion, they demolished tombs, removed religious relics which were kept there, and banned pilgrimage to shrines. On the one hand, the Wahabis wanted to revive the ideal society of early Islam; on the other, they destroyed all historical monuments of the early Islamic history only because people were emotionally attached to them and regarded them as holy and sacred. They implemented strict rules and regulations for observation of religious practices such as praying five times regularly. Those who tried to avoid them were chased by the police (*shurta*) and forced them to go to mosques.

The Wahabi model inspired religious reformers in other Muslim countries and several movements emerged to capture power and reform society on the basis of their religious agenda. In India, the Jihad movement of Sayyid Ahmad Shaheed (d.1831) followed this pattern. To fulfil his mission, he migrated from North India to the North Western Frontier in order to establish his Islamic state there. In 1827, he proclaimed himself as the caliph and Imam. He and his followers used coercive methods to establish a pure and virtuous society in the frontier region. Mirza Hyrat Dehlavi, in his book *Hyat-i-Tayyaba* writes that Sayyid Sahib appointed many of his followers in important posts with the orders that they should force people to follow the *shariat*. However, these officers misused their authority and sometimes forced young girls to marry them. It was also observed that some young holy warriors forcibly took away young ladies from bazaars and streets to mosques and married them without their consent. The officers appointed to look after peasants also misused their power and treated the commonfolk arrogantly. The result was that poor and simple villagers were fed up of their presence. The officers, in order to assert power, declared anybody as *kafir* (unbeliever). If he found somebody's beard larger or longer than his standard, the person's lips were cut off as punishment. If somebody was found wearing *tahmad* (simple cloth to cover the lower body) below the ankles, the bones of his ankles were broken.[12]

We have seen this model in Afghanistan during the rule of the Taliban and in some altered shape in post-revolutionary Iran. It also uses coercive methods to implement its own version of the *shariat*.

IV

In the 19th century, the Islamic world passed through a crisis of colonialism that engulfed it and gradually established political domination in nearly all Muslim countries. The colonial state introduced a new structure of legal system that was quite different from the *shariat*. Colonial states separated religion from politics. Under these circumstances, two types of movements emerged in the Islamic countries: revivalist movements which resisted the colonial state and its hegemony and wanted to implement the *shariat*. Mahdi Sudani's movement in Sudan and the Sannusi movement in Libya worked in this direction. Then there were religious movements whose interest was to create a strong sense of religious identity among the Muslims without involving them in politics. They were not in favour of cooperating with the colonial state. Deoband was its example. In its early period it remained aloof from politics and concentrated on religious teachings and spiritual training of the Muslim community. The Brelvis specially confined their activities to religious rituals.

However, the colonial state and its institutions had a great impact on the social, cultural and economic life of colonised society. Introduction of technology changed the structure of society and behaviour of the people. New ideas of nationalism, socialism, Marxism, and the concept of free market challenged the old customs, traditions and values. Religion was not in a position to respond to these new challenges; therefore, it adopted a defensive policy and failed to take part in the creative process of modern civilisation. When it became stagnant and lost the energy and power to sustain the opposition of modernity, it adopted an ideology of extremism and fundamentalism.[13]

Another important feature of the colonial period was emergence of a European educated class whose model was Europe. They believed in separation of religion and politics. Subsequently religion became the private matter of an individual. Religious attitudes were further affected when there were political movements in the Islamic countries on the basis of nationalism. The character of nationalism was either territorial, linguistic or ethnic. It united people of other religions under the banner of nationalism. For example, in Arab nationalism, the Muslims and Christians were united on a linguistic basis in which the Arabic language became a source of unity and brotherhood.

After decolonisation, when the nation state was established in the former colonies, their constitutions treated all citizens equally irrespective of their colour and creed. State institutions played a neutral role in politics and treated religion as a private matter of individuals. However, in the case of Pakistan the situation was quite different. Attempts were made to transform the new state as Islamic and bring politics and economy under its domination. Religious nationalism excluded people of other religions from its domain and equality of citizenship was affected when the society was divided as the Muslims and non-Muslims. This deprived religious minorities of their basic rights. Religion as a dominant ideology interfered in all aspects of life whether it was economy, education or science and technology.

V

After analysing the impact of different models, we can reach the conclusion that what comes out when religion and politics integrate with each other; and what happens when politics dominates religion or religion subordinates politics. In case of this integration, an absolutist and dictatorial system emerges which saps all creative energies of society and reduces it to passivity. In the case of conflict, both religion and politics use people and their resources in acquiring power and deprive them of social and cultural activities. For example, in today's Saudi Arabia, there is wealth and vast material resources that provide all sorts of comforts and luxuries but there is no culture. Culturally, it is the most backward and barren society. It has not produced any musicians, artists, writers, or filmmakers. It is a society of consumers and not of contributors.

However, whenever, religion is relegated under political, social, or economic pressure, society contributes to philosophy, art and literature, and music. In history such were the periods of the Abbasid rule whose caliph patronised men of letters and scientists. Akbar's reign in the Mughal rule is significant because during this period new ideas were allowed to flourish. Society becomes free when the hold of religion is weak; it becomes barren when religion dominates society and is hostile to all new changes. Society reverts back to old traditions and reduces the role of modernity.

Separation of religion from politics does not make it weak or vulnerable. The real strength of religion lies in the belief of its truthfulness and not in the patronisation and protection of the state. History is evident that whenever, politics is called to help religion, it uses it for its interest and makes an effort to subordinate it which subsequently weakens religion and its beliefs. Moreover, whenever, religion tries to interfere in the economy or politics and cannot keep pace with changes, it becomes the butt of criticism. It is evident that in the modern period there is rapid development in social and natural sciences and religion is not in a position to accommodate all these changes or to interpret them in religious terms. Therefore, the best way is to separate it from politics, economy, and science and technology.

Notes

1. M. Watt, *The Majesty that was Islam*, London, 1974, pp. 108, 120.
2. Al-Mawardi, *al-Ahkam al-Sultaniya* (Urdu translation), Karachi, 1965, p. 66.
3. Abul Fazl, *A'in-i-Akbari*, Calcutta, 1867-1877, A'in, 1, pp. 2, 4.
4. Vanina Eugenia, *Ideas and Society in India from the Sixteenth to Eighteenth Centuries*, OUP, Delhi, 1995, pp. 59, 72.
5. Ziauddin Barani, *Fatawa-i-Jahandari*, Mrs. A. Salim Khan (ed.), Adara-i-Tahqiqat-i-Pakistan wa Danishgah Punjab, Lahore, 1972, pp. 67, 126, 166.
6. Barani, *Tarikh-i-Firuzshahi* (Urdu translation), Markazi Urdu Board, Lahore, 1969, p. 234.
7. *Ibid.*, pp. 378-79.
8. Mubarak Ali, *Ulema aur Siyasat (Ulema and Politics)*, Fiction House, Lahore, 1994, p. 63.
9. Mubarak Ali (ed.), *Aurangzeb Alamgir*, Fiction House, Lahore, 2000, pp. 11-2.
10. Ira Lapidus, *A History of Islamic Societies*, Cambridge, 1988, p. 167.
11. J.A. Merriman, *A History of Modern Europe from the Renaissance to the Present*, Utah, 1988, New York, 1978, Pantheon Islam University Press, p. 119.
12. Mirza Hyrat Dehlavi, *Hayat-i-Tayyaba*, Islami Academy, Urdu Bazar, Lahore, 1976, p. 280.
13. Bassam Tibi, *The Crisis of Modern*, University of Utah Press, 1988, p. 7.

8

Politicisation and Commercialisation of Religion: The Case of Pakistan

When the Muslim League leadership demanded a separate homeland for Indian Muslims, the move was opposed by religious parties such as Jamiat-i-Ulema-i-Hind, Jamaat-i-Islami and the Majlis-i-Ahrar. Their main argument was that the Muslim League leadership was not well versed in matters of religion and consisted of educated but Westernised people not qualified to represent the religious aspirations of the Muslims. As soon as Pakistan came into existence, the Jamaat-i-Islami immediately shifted its headquarters from Pathankot to Lahore, this time with the agenda of turning the newly-created country into a 'truly Islamic' state. Majlis-i-Ahrar, whose leaders mainly belonged to Punjab, focused their attention on launching a movement against the Qadiyanis with the intention of having them declared non-Muslims. (The move resulted in the sectarian conflict of 1954 that discredited the government which failed to control the situation and had to impose martial law in Punjab).

Under such circumstances, Liaquat Ali Khan (d.1951), the prime minister, decided to adopt a strategy of appropriating religion by the state by making the *ulema* redundant and unable to play the religious card. To accomplish this, he invited leading *ulema* from India such as Suleiman Nadvi and Professor Hamidullah to come to Pakistan and help the government evolve a constitution appropriate for a Muslim country. The result of their consultation was not the constitution but the 'Objective Resolutions' which were passed by the legislative assembly in 1949 declaring that 'the sovereignty over [the] entire universe belongs to God Almighty alone and the authority which he has delegated to the State of Pakistan through its people should be exercised within the limits prescribed by Him as a sacred trust'. The Objective Resolutions played an important role in the constitution-making process. All the three constitutions that followed one another declared Pakistan an 'Islamic Republic' with many Islamic provisions. (The Objective Resolutions became a part of the Constitution of 1973 during the dictatorship of Gen. Zia-ul-Haq).

In the first stage, politicisation of Islam was adopted by the ruling classes to capitalise on the religious emotions of the people and consequently an excuse for their own political failures. It was the policy of the state to implement superficial Islamic reforms to satisfy the masses and at the same time to deter the *ulema* from playing an active role in politics. We can call it 'Religious Fundamentalism from above'. However, in the end the idea failed miserably and discredited the state and the ruling classes, both failing to deliver the goods to Pakistan's people. This setback provided an opportunity to the religious parties and the Jamaat-i-Islami, for one, played a decisive though a very destructive and reactionary role in Pakistani politics.

Initially there were two opinions in the Jamaat's circles about its political role: while one group wanted to keep the organisation aloof from politics and 'reform' the society first, the other was in favour of taking part in politics and, after controlling state institutions, implement the *shari'a*. In the end, the latter group prevailed and the Jamaat became more active as a veritable political party. Though successive martial laws did not allow the Jamaat, as a political party, to convince the people of its programme, it was organised with strict discipline and clear programming much in the fashion of a fascist group. In the election of 1970 the party did not fare well. However, during Zia-ul-Haq's regime, it supported the government and helped Zia in his programme of Islamisation. To get the Jamaat's support and cooperation for his military set-up, Zia-ul-Haq held a number of conferences with the *ulema* and *mashaikh* (Sufi saints) participating. At this stage, the state and the *ulema* cooperated with each other in their bid to politicise Islam. Up to this stage, Islam remained a weapon in the hands of the ruling classes and the *ulema* to use it from the above with the help of the state authority. Throughout this period the slogan of Nizam-i-Mustafa (system of governance attributed to the Holy Prophet) was raised to assure the people that the government was sincere in implementing the *sharia* for the people's welfare. One of the important features of this process was the Islamisation of textbooks. Teachers from primary schools to university were instructed to teach every subject, natural sciences as well as social sciences, in the light of Islam. The media also became an active collaborator in this attempt to mould the opinions of people in favour of religious reforms. One of the examples is that the old practice of 'Khuda hafiz' was changed to 'Allah hafiz', which is now prevalent in the Pakistani society. The purpose behind this was to reduce the Persian influence on Pakistani culture and move towards its greater Arabicisation. This process brought religious extremism and narrow mindedness to the doorsteps, even inside the homes, of the masses.

However, the situation changed drastically in the 1980s as a result of the Afghan '*jihad*'. The arrival of the Russian army in Afghanistan alarmed the United States of the communist peril. To counter it, the *jihad* movement was launched by the American government. The CIA became active and its 'operation cyclone' involved nearly 7 billion dollars to ISI to help the *mujahedeen*. Another 2 billion dollars were given directly to various Afghan factions. Added to this 10 billion dollars as joint Saudi-CIA cash aid for 'covert operations'.[1] The University of Nebraska, especially, prepared textbooks for the students glorifying the *jihad*.

Huge funding from the United States and the oil-rich Arab countries changed the whole scenario in Pakistan and phenomenally increased the number of religious parties. In the 1970s, there were only 30 religious parties. In the 1980s their number rose to 237.[2] All these religious parties and groups benefited from foreign funding as well as received a tangible amount from *Zakat* collected by the state. The new mushrooming *jihadi* organisations, in order to get more funds, required more volunteers and a more active role in Afghanistan. That was the beginning of 'commercialisation of religion'. The *jihad* movements were now big corporations or business houses. This also created competition among the *jihadi* groups. In the early stages there were a few organisations who were involved in the holy war against the Russian infidels. As the business flourished, there was division and several splinter groups emerged to play an independent role in the *jihad*. The reason behind the division was that every religious leader now wanted to become solely in charge of a group and use the fund at his own discretion. Further, every group wanted to assert its importance in the *jihad* and take credit for all victories against the enemy. One example is the division of the Harkatul Mujahedin. The group which splintered from it called itself 'Jesh-i-Muhammad' (army of the Holy Prophet) and demanded its share from funding. The new splinter group also claimed all those who were killed in Afghanistan and Kashmir as its own militants.[3] This indicates how these groups exploited the dead to achieve their own goals.

The emergence of the *jihadi* movements undermined the role of the politico-religious parties. As most of these parties were reformist in nature and had wanted to acquire power within the existing political structure, their support and power base was the urban educated middle class which was intellectually impressed by the writings of Abul Ala Maudoodi and Sayyid Qutb from Egypt. The *jihadi* movements, on the other hand, were radical and wanted to revolutionise the whole Muslim world by their act of *jihad*. Their volunteers were mostly from rural areas and semi-educated. Their focus was not the internal politics of Pakistan but fighting the enemies in Afghanistan and Kashmir. To attract the young people from the villages and small towns, they set up their offices and *madaris* (religious schools) throughout the country. Before the 1980s, the number of *madaris* was 700. The Afghan war increased the number up to 10,000. The method which was adopted to mobilise young students was to exaggerate the Muslims' ordeal as a result of oppression by the Russians, the Jews and the Hindus. They were told that the only way to liberate the Muslims was *jihad*. Young volunteers were encouraged to fulfil the divine mission and lay down their lives for a higher religious cause.

The significant features of the *jihadi* culture which were popularised as a result of the activities of the *jihadi* organisations were: first, the name of these groups indicated their *jihadi* character such as Harkatul Mujahedin (movement of the holy warriors), Harkatul jihad al Islami Pakistan (movement of Islamic holy war of Pakistan), Jesh-i-Muhammad (army of the Holy Prophet), Jamiatul Mujahedin al Aalami, (world organisation of holy warriors), Jamat Dawa (organisation for preaching), and Lashkar-i-Tayyaba (army of puritans). Some of these groups confined their activities only to Afghanistan and Kashmir and some of them even send *jihadis* to Chechnya and Bosnia to fight along with the local fighters.

These groups also derived their *jihadi* inspiration from the past Muslim history. Some of the radical groups were

named Al-badr (crescent, an Islamic symbol), Al-barq (lighting) and Al-mahajarun (immigrants). Some of them called their volunteers *Fadai* (derived from loyalists belonging to the Ismaili leader Hasan bin Sabah on whose orders they were prepared to sacrifice their lives).They named their training camps after those historical personalities who had fought against non-Muslims such as Muhammad bin Qasim, the Arab conqueror of Sindh, Mahmud of Ghazni, who invaded India and demolished a number of Hindu temples, Sayyid Ahmad Shaheed and Ismail Shaheed, who were the leaders of the *jihad* movement against the Sikhs in the 19th century and were killed at Balakot in 1831.

The *jihadi* organisations used modern technology extensively to propagate their views. *Madaris* and mosques were the institutions which became their centres of activities. Newspapers, magazines, pamphlets, exhibitions, demonstrations, public meetings, cassettes and videos were the instruments which were adopted by all parties to popularise their image as the true and successful *jihadi* movement. The names of their newspapers and magazines also indicated their *jihadi* trends. For example, some of the names were Zarb-i momin (striking of the believer), Sada-i-jihad (voice of holy war) Sut-i-Kashmir (voice of Kashmir) Sada-i-Mujahid (voice of holy warrior) and Shamshir (sword).

To encourage the volunteers to fight and acquire the status of martyrs, the *jihadi* movements popularised their own culture of mourning. When a young *mujahid* died in Kashmir or Afghanistan, the concerned group, instead of condolence, congratulated the family of the deceased on the martyrdom of their relative. Such was the pressure of the culture that if somebody visited for condolence, the family rebuked him and said proudly that it was the moment of pride and happiness for them that their son/brother died for a sacred cause. People, instead of condolence, should congratulate them. Soon, everybody accepted it and on the occasion of the news the relatives and friends garlanded the family of the martyr and distributed sweets to celebrate it. It also became a custom that the street where the family of the dead *mujahid* lived was named after the martyr. The religious interpretation of this culture was that martyrs never die; they live an eternal life, therefore, their departure from this world should be celebrated.

The characteristic of this culture is that personal grief is not important. The grief of an individual is the pride of a community. The martyr no more remains the property of the family but of his organisation. And by celebrating martyrdom, it inspires others to emulate him and desire for the glorious death. However, the tragic part of this culture is that the family has to endure its sorrow and grief privately and mourn the death silently. In case of natural death there are no such rituals.[4]

The *jihadi* movements for the first time raised the social status of the *ulema*. Once they got plenty of funds, the *jihadi* leaders also changed their personal lifestyles and adopted social symbols meant to impress the others such as landcruisers, jeeps and other costly cars, armed guards, air conditioned houses and offices. The support of the government agencies also made them influential in the ruling circles.

However, this situation has somewhat changed after 9/11. The regime change in Afghanistan, and the campaign by Pakistan to fight terrorism have radically undermined the role of the *jihadi* groups. The government under international pressure banned the *jihadi* parties and tried to stop their foreign funding. As a result, these groups either changed their names or went underground. It appears that in the present political development they are becoming irrelevant with no *jihad* in Afghanistan. There is let-up on the Kashmir issue also because of the peace negotiations between India and Pakistan. There is a possibility that having no funds, no support from the ruling classes, and no issue for *jihad*, these groups will disappear gradually as they never had any popular base in Pakistan in any case.

Notes

1. For further details see, Mary Anne Weaver, *Pakistan in the Shadow of Jihad and Afghanistan*, Farrar & Group, New York, 2002.
2. Muhammad Aamir Rana, *Jihad-i-Kashmir War Afghanistan*, Lahore, 2002, p. 49.
3. *Ibid.*, p. 147.
4. Mubarak Ali, 'War Heroes and Mourning Hypocrisy', in *A Page from History*, 2004, pp. 77-8.

9

Karachi: Living City, Dying Culture

Thus the very traits that have made the metropolis always seem at once alien and hostile to the folk in the hinterland are an essential part of the big city's function. It has brought together, within a relatively narrow compass, the diversity and variety of special cultures: at least in token quantities all races and cultures can be found here, along with their languages, their customs, their costumes, their typical cuisines: here the representatives of mankind first met face to face on neutral ground. The complexity and the cultural inclusiveness of the metropolis embody the complexity of the great capitals have been preparing mankind for the wider associations and unifications which the modern conquest of time and space has made probable, if not inevitable.[1]

Every city has two characteristics: its ancientness and its historicity. Ancientness of any city is determined on the basis of archaeological evidence. When this evidence remains inconclusive, ancient history becomes a fertile ground of legends and myths. Historians, in the absence of facts, construct a mythical history on the basis of speculation and imagination. On the other hand, the historicity of a city is determined on written documentary evidence. Analysis and examination of documents help historians to draw a comprehensive picture of a city. The city becomes historical only when it contributes to politics, literature, economics, and culture and creates its own soul, which distinguishes it from others. It also assumes significance because of its geographical and strategical location.

Throughout history cities became prominent and famous either because of their political and commercial importance or their cultural and social contribution to society. Those cities, which remained capitals of an empire or administrative centres, assumed an authoritative and hierarchical character, but those cities, which were centres of trade and commerce, developed a homogeneous culture without much political domination and supervision.

Residential areas of the cities of the Indian subcontinent were divided on the basis of ethnicity, religion, caste, and linguistic affiliations. There were separate places of worship and centres for social gatherings to keep their religious and ethnic identities, but once they came out from their residential space to the public space such as markets, gardens, playgrounds, working places, and government offices, they came into contact with each other. Interaction, meeting, exchange of ideas in public space created a sense of belonging to the city which united and combined their interests. That was the sense of belonging that people defended their city with equal zeal and faced crises and vicissitudes of politics with patience. In such a milieu, a city created its traditions, customs, rituals, and festivals, which culminated in the creation of its unique character.

Karachi is not an ancient town. And so it has no historical monuments and no archaeological remains. It was a small and an insignificant fishermen's town that was developed in 1729 by a Hindu merchant Bhojomal as a port. The city passed through three historical stages. In the early period of history it remained a part of Balochistan and Sindh; in the second stage it was occupied by the British in 1839; and finally in 1947 it became the first capital of the newly independent country of Pakistan. In all these three stages the city assumed different and distinct characters. In the first stage, it remained an insignificant port of Sindh. During the colonial period it became one of the cleanest cities and developed a culture of tolerance, humanism, and enlightenment. After partition the whole landscape of the city changed and new emigrants from India brought a new culture to the city and made it a mini India. In the later period when the Pathans, Punjabis, and Balochis arrived in search of jobs and economic opportunities, the city became mini Pakistan. The history of Karachi during all these stages on the one hand is fascinating, but on the other hand, very sad. In this paper an attempt is made to capture the spirit of the city and highlight its main features and characteristics.

I

In 1839, T.G. Carless visited Karachi and submitted his observations to the government. He writes:

> The town of Kurachee is built upon a slightly elevated piece of ground, which projects a short distance into swamps and flats on the eastern side of the harbour. It occupies rather a large space, and is defended by a mud wall, with round towers at each angle, and along the sides. The fortifications, however, are of meanest description, and are in the most dilapidated state: most of the towers are merely heaps of earth, ...Like most native cities the space inside is completely filled up with houses, and the streets are so narrow that two horsemen can barely pass each other in the principal thoroughfares.... At present Kurachee has a population of 14,000 souls, half of which are Hindoos, and the rest Baloochees, Jokeeaahe, Mowannas, and Jutts. Many of the Hindoo merchants possess great wealth, and as a body they are more independent, and possess great influence, as any other part of Sind. This arises from the desire of their rulers to increase the tradė of the port, and encourage those who, in the course of their mercantile pursuits, contribute so largely to the revenue of the country.[2]

In its early and first phase Karachi remained not only an insignificant town but also lack of sanitation made it dirty. There was no concept of town planning, so the town grew haphazardly. Richard Burton who visited the town somewhere in 1844 leaves an interesting account of it:

Karachi town, when I first became acquainted with it, was much like the Alexandria of a century and a half ago: a few tenements of stone and lime emerging from a mass of low hovels, mat and mud, and of tall mud houses with windowless mud walls, flat mud roofs, and many Bad-girs or mud ventilators, surrounded by tumble platform of mud covered rock...On approaching it, three organs were affected, far more powerfully, however, than pleasantly, viz., the ear, the nose, and the eye. The former was struck by tomtoming and squeaking of native music; by roaring, bawling, criard voices of the people; by barking and braying of stranger-hating curs, and by screams of hungry gulls fighting over scraps of tainted fish. The drainage, if you could so call it, was managed by evaporation: every one threw before his dwelling what was not wanted inside, while dogs, kites, and crows were the only scavengers; and this odour of carrion was varied, as we approached the bazars, by a close, faint, dead smell of drugs and spices, such as might be supposed to proceed from newly made 'Osiris'.[3]

The town did not develop because of lack of interest of the Talpur rulers who neither had resources nor vision. The wealthy merchants of the city also had no concept of town planning and no desire to improve it. This shows cultural backwardness and absence of social awareness of the rich and resourceful inhabitants of the town.

II

After the conquest of Sindh (1843), in 1847 it became a part of the Bombay Presidency. The British administration gave particular attention to the development of Karachi and gradually it transformed from an unknown and sleepy town to a prominent city of the Indian subcontinent. It became a modern and well planned city. By the time the British conquered Sindh, they had already experience of town planning. In 19th century Europe, as a result of industrialisation and commercial activities, the bourgeoisie or burgher class developed their cities taking care to provide more space for public utilities and entertainment. That is why, besides administrative buildings such as courts, post offices, railway stations, town halls, government offices, there were gardens, theatres, galleries, museums, elegant shopping arcades, clubs, cafes to provide space to the citizens to enjoy themselves and relax. For public utilities there were hospitals, educational institutions, libraries, banks, workhouses for poor and churches. There were wide roads, avenues, and thoroughfares that facilitated the transport. A system of sanitation and disposal of waste kept cities clean. The municipality took the administration under the mayor to keep the city in order. Another important feature of the new city structure was its secular character. In the medieval cities of Europe, the cathedral used to be in the centre of the city; in the new structure commercial buildings became the centre symbolising secularism over religion.

Based on this experience, the British developed Calcutta, Madras and Bombay. They applied this experience in the development of Karachi as a modern port city. After the conquest, the pattern of Karachi's population had also changed. Once it developed as a port city; it attracted the business communities from all over India. They came in search of new opportunities to earn more wealth. So, here came the Memons, Bohris, Kacchis, Parsis, Khojas, Marwaris, Malabaris, and Goans from the island of Goa, Europeans and even some Jews. Arrival of these communities made the city multi-ethnic, multi-cultural, and multi-religious. These communities on the one hand maintained their separate identity, but on the other, they influenced each other culturally and socially which resulted in a homogenised culture based on secularism and tolerance.

These communities, after adopting the city of Karachi as their permanent settlement, developed a great sense of belonging that created a strong desire and urge to make it special and unique. The Parsi community played an active role in the development especially during the period of Jamshid Nasarvanji Mehta who served as the president of the municipality from 1921 to 1933. During this period sanitation was improved, supply of water was regulated, roads were repaired, gardens were laid out, maternity homes were built, new housing schemes were started to solve the problem of housing, and a majestic municipal building was constructed. As a result of his efforts the city got a new look. It became a model of cleanliness.

Karachi emerged as a trading and commercial and not as an industrial town. This saved it from pollution and also from slums. The population did not increase rapidly and remained under control. Before the British conquest the population was only 14,000. According to the census of 1881, it was 73,560; in 1891 it was 10,5199, and before the partition it was 3,86,655. The small population helped the city administration to keep it peaceful and clean.

The types of buildings that were built in the modern city show their commercial, educational, administrative, and recreational values. The commercial interests kept religious and ethnic differences far behind. The trading communities, after earning wealth, instead of hoarding and spending it on their personal comfort and luxury, denote a considerable portion of it for welfare and charitable work.

One of its examples is the Parsi community. It earned a respect in the society by its contribution to public and charitable work. The tradition of social work brought wealthy people into contact with the poor. It provided them opportunities to understand their deprivation and problems.

This led to the alleviation of their grievances. Humanism and tolerance was the result of social work. That is why the theosophical movement led by Annie Besant also influenced some of the leading figures of the city. This created such an atmosphere that not only human beings but animals were also tendered and cared for. Pir Ali Rashidi, a politician and writer of the Sindhi language, in his memoirs writes about the humanitarian culture of Karachi before partition and how the people of Karachi cared for the rights of animals. If anybody was caught beating animals, he was charged and fined. Cart drivers were not allowed to accommodate more passengers than fixed by the law. There were societies for animal protection whose office holders were honorary magistrates; it was their task to keep an eye on owners of cart and carriage drivers not to treat animals harshly. If somebody was found treating them badly he was either reprimanded or fined. There were hospitals for old and sick animals. There were a number of troughs in the city where cool water was available for the animals. The Parsis in memory of their ancestors built most of these troughs. The Hindus also maintained *gaoshalas* for old animals. He relates his personal experience when he visited Karachi:

> It was around 1930 that I was passing Bandar road. Suddenly I saw Jamshed Mehta taking a wounded donkey to hospital. His car and driver were coming behind him slowly. I also followed him and, after reaching to the hospital, waited to see the proceedings. The doctor cleaned the wounds and bandaged the donkey in the presence of Jamshed. He was very much concerned and requested the doctor to clean the wounds carefully so as not to give any pain to the animal. After it, he asked the doctor to keep the donkey in hospital at his own expense. He also gave advance money for fodder for the animal. He then turned to the owner and asked him not to take it from the hospital as long as it recovered fully. To compensate the man he gave him some money.[4]

However, the development of Karachi was in contrast to rural Sindh where the strong domination of feudals kept the society backward and stagnant. The contrast showed the attitudes of feudals and trading communities. Karachi became a cultural, educated, and commercial town, while rural Sindh remained socially and culturally far behind.

To the people of rural Sindh to visit Karachi was to visit some foreign city. The environment of the city created awe and fear among the arrivals of the rural areas. Rashidi aptly depicts this:

When people saw the shops of Elphinstone Street they felt a sense of inferiority. Except for a few shops of Memons all the others belonged to the English, Parsis, and Hindu Amils...When they decided to enter the shop first they cleaned their shoes, buttoned their coats, and put in order their moustaches and beards by running their hands over them. All this done fearing that they might not have any encounter with the Englishmen in the shop.[5]

Similarly, they also avoided encounters with the English women (memsahibs or madams). Rashidi relates an event when he saw a feudal from Jacobabad hiding himself along with his servants in a shop. On his inquiry he told him:

Shah sahib we do not know to which officers these women belong. We heard that in this area there are bungalows of the commissioner, collector and other senior officials. If any madam does not like our group wandering in this area, she would send us to jail. We come here to enjoy ourselves and not to face tigers and wolves. It is better to remain away from these people.[6]

Rashidi's description of the city is charming. He writes about trams that transported passengers from Saddar to Kemari. It cost only one taka. Travelling was comfortable. There were no crowds, no rush; everybody could get a seat. Besides trams there were horse drawn carriages. Wealthy people used to have Victoria carriages for their personal use. He writes about the first car owner:

Seth Abdur Rahim Saleh Muhammad imported the first motor car. That was Humber without any roof. When it came out on the road people stood on the side with respect. The British generally liked horse riding; they used to go to Clifton to have fresh air. The road was still not built properly. I have often seen the commissioner Sir Lawrence going to Clifton with his wife without any guard or escort.[7]

That was the colonial Karachi

III

A new Karachi emerged after the partition of 1947 when it became the capital of a new country. There came new arrivals from all parts of India and brought along with them their culture and their regional traditions and customs. They also brought the memories of their cities, towns, and villages and transformed Karachi into mini India. They named their new settlements and residential areas after their ancestral cities and provinces. There is Bihar colony, Benglore town, Rajputana colony, Ajmer Nagri, and Aligarh colony to name a few. Similarly, one can see the names of shops as Delhi hotel, Ambala sweetmeat, Pilibhit Oil Company, Jaipur hair cutting salon, and Agra shoe shop. Names of roads were also decolonised, for example Victoria road became Abdullah Haroon road, Napier road as Mir Karam Ali Talpur road, Nathal bhai Patel road as Nawab Ismail Khan, and Lawrence road as Nishtar road, Elphinston street as Zaibunisa street, Motilal Nehru road as Jigar Muradabadi road, and Connaught road as Chaudhary Rahmat Ali road. Those individuals who were honoured in this way did not contribute to the development of Karachi. The selection shows that most of them were politicians and not social workers. It was an indication that, in the new set up, politics was more important than social work. It also shows that there was no place either for the British or the Hindus in the new set up of the city. All statues of the colonial period that graced the city disappeared from the scene.

The new emigrants brought strong religious and political prejudices. They adopted the country as their new homeland on the basis of Islamic ideology; although most of them came either as government servants or with the hope to find new economic opportunities or as a result of communal riots in their areas. However, they showed their deep attachment to religion and new political ideology in which there was no space for others. As they came in large numbers, they pushed the old inhabitants of Karachi into the background. A strong bureaucracy curtailed the power of the municpality. The commissioner of Karachi ruled like an uncrowned king. The evacuee property was allotted indiscriminately. It changed the whole landscape of the city. Soon well educated and wealthy Hindus left Karachi. The Parsis relegated their prominent position and retired. The followers of other faiths such as the Sikhs and the Jews disappeared. Karachi was given a new look: a number of mosques were built throughout the city that asserted the domination of religion on other aspects of society. Karachi no longer remained a multi-cultural or multi-religious city. Religious tolerance was taken over by religious fanaticism. Humanism was replaced by rigidity. With the increase of population, the old infrastructure collapsed. It was neither replaced by a new one nor it was improved.

However, the Mohajirs or refugees planted a new culture in the city. Urdu became the language of daily use. The tradition of Mushai'ra was revived and popularised in the new cultural milieu. Religious festivals such as Moharram procession and Milad (birth of the holy Prophet) were celebrated with religious fervour. Urdu magazines, newspapers and books began to be published. Some of the great literary figures such as Josh Malihabadi, Niaz Fatehpuri, Shahid Ahmad Dehlavi and others rejuvenated literary activities. As there were no restrictions on the Indian visitors to visit Pakistan till 1965, so famous and popular poets, religious scholars used to visit Karachi regularly. These contacts maintained cultural links with India. Those literary people who published their memoirs recall their Indian past with sadness. There are intense feelings of losing the past.

Arif Hassan, a city planner and writer recalls the early days of Karachi after the partition. He is of the opinion that the arrival of the Mohajirs created a fertile ground for intellectual activities in Karachi. In the early period they settled around the Saddar, a central area of the city. Among the new arrivals were bureaucrats, poets, painters, and musicians. Saddar became the centre of their activities. Up to 1965, in the Saddar area there were 37 eating places, 9 bars, 11 billiard rooms, 18 book shops, 7 auditoriums and 4 disco clubs. Seminars on literary and academic topics, variety shows, and debates that attracted a large number of interested people were organised regularly. India Coffee House became the centre of students and politicians where debates and discussions on politics and current affairs went on unending. He also remembers Capital and Paradise cinemas where film festivals were held. There were Karachi Goan Club and Sohrab Katrak halls which were famous for their cultural and social activities. The Parsi Gymkhana and Goan Gymkhana organised sports competitions. He recalls that there was a time when the area of Saddar was a pleasant place to walk and to meet friends.[8]

In the 1960s, Karachi was politically very active. The students' community was against Ayub Khan and his martial law. Demonstrations, strikes, and processions of students mobilised the city's general public against the government. Ayub Khan used all coercive methods to crush the opposition. Some student leaders were banished from the city; some of them were put in prison, but the opposition continued. His government then decided to shift the capital from Karachi to Islamabad, a safe place from any demonstration or protest. The shifting of capital purified Karachi from bureaucracy and the presence of ruling classes. It now assumed a new identity and that was its commercial and industrial transformation

IV

The process of industrialisation began just after the partition. When new industries were set up, there was requirement of cheap labour. Unemployment and lack of development compelled people from the North West Frontier Province and the Punjab to come to Karachi. The arrivals of newcomers slowly changed the population pattern of the city. Now, Karachi assumed a new identity. It became 'mini Pakistan'. There emerged new settlements of the Pathans and Punjabis. They brought their own culture and way of life. The Pathans came along with their tribal values and Jirga system and the Punjabis with their boldness and enterprise. The Mohajirs resented this intrusion. They felt threatened and resisted sharing with any ethnic group.

In 1970, when One Unit was abolished and Karachi became the capital of Sindh province, it brought Sindhi administration and politicians to Karachi. So far the Sindhi population of the city was in the background and not in a position to assert its existence. The Mohajir community that so long enjoyed the monopoly in the city became unnerved to lose its power. These feelings ultimately caused the emergence of the Mohajir Quomi Movement. Moreover, the political development of Pakistan greatly affected the city. The Karachi Corporation became a bureaucratic institution. It no longer remained an elective body. Besides, people of other provinces and many Afghans, Bengalis, Burmese, and Iranis came illegally and settled there. As most of them are unskilled workers and have a rural background, their attitude and beheviour is no match for the for middle class culture of the Mohajirs. It resulted in a number of ethnic clashes. The result is that the culture of 'mini India' which was so enthusiastically planted and nurtured was uprooted and swept away by the new waves of immigration and with the emergence of 'mini Pakistan'.

In spite of all these changes, Karachi is identified as a Mohajir city. The rural Sindh poses hostility to the city as it divided the province culturally and ethnically. The communities who belong to other provinces have their social links with their ancestral homes. The Mohajirs, after delinking their relations with India, are locked in the city without any hinterland support. Their separate Mohajir identity is not recognised by any ethnic group of Pakistan. As a result the city has suffered. There is no sense of belonging to the city. That is why unplanned new high rise buildings and plazas have disfigured the city. Old buildings and monuments are in a state of dilapidation. There is no interest to preserve them; as all newcomers disown the city's past.

Change is inevitable. Cities also change with the passage of time. However, if change causes deterioration of the city and makes life unbearable, the past haunts people. In the case of Karachi, the tragedy is that the past of this city haunts only a few people who lived before the partition in this city of peace, prosperity and homogenised culture. But most of them live without any memories of the past.

Notes

1. Lewis Mumford, *The City in History,* Penguin Books, 1976, p. 639.
2. T.G. Carless, 'Memoirs on the Bay, Harbour, and Trade, of Kurachee', in *Memoirs of Sindh,* Hughes Thomas, Vol. I, Delhi, 1993, p. 196.
3. R. Burton, *Sindh Revisited,* Vol. I-II, Karachi, 1993, pp. 45-6.
4. Pir Ali Muhammad Rashid, *Wo Din Wo Log* (*Those Days, Those People*), in *Aaj,* Autumn, 1995, pp. 101-02.
5. *Ibid.,* p. 104.
6. *Ibid.,* p. 106.
7. *Ibid.,* p. 134.
8. Arif Hasan, 'Karachi City', in *Aaj,* Autumn, 1995, pp. 390-91.

Index